Sakhnin

Portrait of an Environmental Peace Project in Israel

Jan Martin Bang

Floris Books

First published in 2009 by Floris Books, Edinburgh

www.florisbooks.co.uk

British Library CIP Data available

ISBN 978-086315-686-1

Printed in Singapore

Contents

Acknowledgments

My first and biggest debt of gratitude must go to my wife, Ruth Wilson. She did so much of the work that went into writing this book that she is pretty much a co-author. She took the notes at every interview, building up the raw material from which the book was written. She went through the text, correcting and improving. She created a space for me where I could concentrate on my part of the work. It was our first writing collaboration, and it was a joy to work together. Thank you, Ruth!

Our children saw us disappearing south in a red VW camper, to return a year later. Thank you for putting up with our quest for adventure, and for being there upon our return.

Our community at Camphill Solborg gave us a sabbatical year's leave of absence, without which it would have been impossible to spend the time we needed at Sakhnin. Thank you for this support.

The people of Sakhnin welcomed us with open arms, especially Hussein Tarabeah, his wife Giselle Hasan and their children Adi, Anan and Joule. We have known them for many years. Working on this book and living in Sakhnin has deepened, strengthened and consolidated the bonds between our two families. The staff at the environmental centre, and the many people we visited in Sakhnin welcomed us into their homes, showered us with both gifts and acts of kindness, and I can only say that it was an experience that we shall look back on with pleasure and gratefulness.

I would like to thank the following by name, for the time they set aside for us, and the stories they told us: Hussein Tarabeah, Shlomo

Kimchie, Saleh Waked, Mukhles Hajouj, Hanadi Hijris, Said Khalaili, Bassem Ganaim, Riyad Dwere, Khuzam Zriek, Jummana Essa, Yussuf Ganaim, Mustafa Abu Raya, Jamal Tarabeah, Eitan Rozenberg, Amin Abu Raya, Haim Shinhar, Abed Yassen, Haggai Raban, Jonatan Ritter, Laithi Ganaim, Ahmad Hag, Badria Biromi-Kandalaft, Rafeh Abu Raya, Abed Al Majed, Gasan Ganaim and Yuval Steinberg.

I must also mention with thanks Panos Baltos and Despina Papaioannou of the Ariadne Foundation in Greece for providing me with a quiet place on which to work on this book.

This is the third book that I have published through Floris Books, and it confirms to me that a close and collaborative co-operation with a publisher is the key to success. Thank you, Christian Maclean, the rest of the staff at Floris Books, and especially my editor Christopher Moore for his endless patience and hard work in taking my ideas and translating them into a product that hopefully will be enjoyed by many.

Lastly, but most importantly, I want to thank all those who work for peace in the Middle East, and indeed in all of the troubled conflict areas of our planet. You are the unsung heroes, usually passed over by the mass media. Your contribution to the welfare of humanity is priceless. I dedicate this book to you.

Introduction

I have been connected to the Middle East and Israel for most of my adult life. I have spent nearly two years as a volunteer on kibbutz, and sixteen years as a member of Kibbutz Gezer, where my children grew up. During that time I have watched the region slide into a constantly increasing spiral of violence. In the 1980s I naively thought that if I came to live here, voted for peace parties in elections and participated in Israeli-Palestinian dialogue, peace would come.

It didn't.

It was only when I began to study the writings of Rudolf Steiner, specifically his theory of social threefolding, that I saw what was missing. This was introduced by Steiner as part of his general teachings in Anthroposophy in lectures during the last part of the First World War and the years that followed. He based his thoughts on his study of the development of European society over the preceding centuries. In England, he saw the industrial revolution as the modernization of economic life, leading to demands for *fraternity*, the development of trade unionism and labour party politics. In France under the French Revolution he saw a change in the legal life leading to demands for *equality*, and in Middle Europe (later unified to become Germany) changes in the spiritual life leading to demands for *liberty*. I like to think of this as the social application of anthroposophy.

Steiner traced how these three great ideals, of fraternity, equality and liberty, had been corrupted by the rise of nationalism and the development of the centralized nation state. The threefold analysis was conceived by Steiner as a way of rebuilding Europe after the disaster of the First World War, but his ideas did not gain credence, and the ideas were largely dormant until taken up by other anthroposophists.

In a lecture I attended a few years ago by the leading Israeli anthroposophist, Yishiyahu Ben Aharon, I first heard of threefolding being applied to peacework. Just as a healthy society needs a clear balance between equality in politics, fellowship in economics and freedom in culture, so does a successful peace process need to include dialogue and co-operation in all three aspects. Yishiyahu showed me how the Oslo peace process didn't succeed because it was only a political process, and not enough progress was made on economic and cultural coexistence.

This book is an attempt to show that peacework in the field of education and cultural dialogue is still going on, even if the political process has stopped, and the economics of peace never really got off the ground. It is also my intention to balance the violent, depressing picture that we are generally served by the mass media. My frequent visits and my many years of living in Israel have brought me into contact with very many fine people, people who want to live in peace, people who spend a great deal of their time, most of it unpaid, to bring Jews and Arabs together, to build peace from the ground up. I wanted to describe something of this in detail, introducing a cast of real live characters, to show an attempt to solve social and political problems.

For many years I worked at teaching, inspiring and helping environmental projects in Israel and it was during this time that I first met Hussein Tarabeah. Learning and teaching Permaculture I was aware of the principle of 'turning a problem into a solution'. Sewage was the problem. Encouraging Arabs and Jews to work together on sewage treatment was the solution. Peace could be the result. Such a simple formula! It caught my imagination, and inspired this book.

I try as much as possible to refer to the environmental centre at Sakhnin as TAEQ throughout the book. This is an acronym for Towns Association for Environmental Quality, a pretty poor translation of the Hebrew *Igud Arim L Ichut HaSviva,* but it is at least correct according to the dictionary. Sometimes, for variety, I will refer to it as the Centre. In spelling place names generally I have tried to keep to the forms used in the Mapa atlases published in Israel, possibly the most popular English language atlas. With Arabic and Hebrew names I have used the form that the individuals preferred, and tried to be consistent.

Land in Israel is measured in dunam, which is part of the legal inheritance from the Ottoman Turks. The plural of dunam is also dunam, and 1 dunam equals 0.25 acres. For English speakers, this means that 4 dunam is 1 acre. For those who prefer metric measurements, 10 dunam equals 1 hectare.

As an English speaker with only mediocre Hebrew and non-existent Arab literacy, documentary research was out of the question, apart from a few brochures and grant proposals available at TAEQ. I tried to turn this handicap into an advantage, and decided to concentrate on presenting a picture built up by the people involved or affected by the project. My information is based upon personal interviews, and rather than try to give an objective account, I wanted to present a picture of how these people see themselves, their history and their involvement. In the shifting sands of the Middle East, truth is difficult to catch, as it flits from dune to dune. But there is a personal, tribal and national truth in how people see themselves, even if others may perceive them differently. These are the pictures I wanted to capture.

Galilee

The Middle East

1. The Valley of Sakhnin

The Valley of Sakhnin lies in the centre of Galilee, and from many of the mountains around it your eye travels from sea to sea, from the Mediterranean to the Sea of Galilee. Many people who live here think of this as the original Garden of Eden, and with mild winters, warm summers and flowers all year round, it's hard to disagree. Over ten thousand years ago, agriculture was invented somewhere in this region, which later spread over the whole planet, completely changing our way of life. No longer were we hunter gatherers.

A local archaeologist told us that originally this area was named Saganim, from a group of workers who came from Egypt. It was famous for the pink dye that comes from snails found in Nahal Hilazon, one of the rivers draining the valley. In 600 BC Sakhnin was called Sagan, the Persian name for a rank in their army. Later it came to be called Sakhani, related to a word for oil. To this day many maintain that they have the best olives here. In those far-off Second Temple times, Jews lived here and, in nearby Araba, Jewish graves from this period have been found. Sakhnin appears in the writings of Josephus, but it was completely destroyed by the Romans. In Byzantine times, before Islam, tribes moved into the area, including the family of Abu Raya and Tarabeah. We shall meet contemporary members of these families throughout the book.

There is an ancient grave here in Sakhnin, reputed by some to be of the holy man, Rabbi Yehoshua of Sakhnin. There is no doubt that he existed, but it is difficult to say whether this really is his grave. Judging by the stones used and the way in which it was built the grave is certainly very old. The grave faces north-south, so it is definitely not Muslim, but it could be Jewish or Christian. He is called by the Hebrew term *Tzaddik* by locals, and the grave is seen as a holy place by everyone. Muslims take the Koran there if they need to swear by something. Both Muslims and Jews have a tradition of tying ribbons to the trees next to the grave as recognition of wishes granted or prayers answered.

During Crusader times there were no serious battles around Sakhnin. However, Saladin (Salah ad-Din) was sometimes in the area and there is a huge pistachio tree in the Beit Netofa Valley where he reputedly hid and nursed his wounds. Sakhnin was already a Muslim town by this time. Abu el-Hija from the nearby village of Kaukab fought for Saladin, was killed and buried there, and his grave survives to this day.

Later the Turks came and greatly affected the Arab culture. Sakhnin was already a well recognized place by then. The Ottoman Turks granted a good deal of freedom as long as they were paid their taxes. They were not concerned with religious coercion. Around 1800 a student from Sakhnin, Mussa Abu Raya, was studying at a school in Akko and was chosen to go to Mecca with Al Jazar, a great tribal leader and founder of the school. When Mussa returned he built a house which is now home to the Museum of Palestinian Heritage in Sakhnin. In addition he received gifts of land, including Deir al-Asad, Kabul, Araba, and as far north as the present Lebanese border. Mussa later became a judge and rose in power. Sakhnin grew to become the centre of the Galilee, in an area with a wide range of different families and tribes; Muslims, Christians, Druze, Bedouin and Sufis, each with their own culture, religion, history and customs.

The Arabs call this region *Lmal,* perhaps related to the name for the common oak. It is a symbol for a people who have their roots in the land. According to the locals, Sakhnin has an ancient tradition of welcoming outsiders, more than other places around here. This is certainly something we could agree with. In our experience the inhabitants of Sakhnin carried on living up to their reputation.

Before the establishment of the State of Israel in 1948, agriculture was simple here and life was hard. People raised goats, chickens, cows, donkeys and camels. There was a good deal of trading between British Mandate Palestine and the Lebanon, but the British would sometimes come and kill goats to feed their soldiers.

As well as farming the land in the Sakhnin Valley, many people owned land in Beit Netofa, an hour away by donkey or camel.

There the land is divided up according to the Muslim tradition, where each child is apportioned a subdivided plot of land. Seen from the surrounding hills, this gives a coloured carpet effect of yellows, greens and browns. A good deal of rain washes down into the valley during the winter, and there are periodic floods. However, the valley never received water from the Sea of Galilee when the government dug a canal through it to pipe it down to the Negev. Some regard this as a political decision to hinder development of a primarily Arab area.

Later, a road was opened from Sakhnin and Araba to Beit Netofa, and as the area developed the farmers began to think in terms of industrial agriculture such as sugar beet. Until 1980 most people here worked in agriculture, with olives in the Sakhnin Valley and other crops in the Netofa Valley. But, by the mid-1980s people began to leave agriculture and went to work elsewhere. This would in the long term have led to a deterioration of the environment, but already people are again beginning to return. The direction which agriculture will take in this area is something which we shall return to in a later chapter.

During the British Mandate, Sakhnin remained largely peaceful. Apart from some individuals, people were not interested in fighting either the British or the Jews. In 1948 Sakhnin was one of the few towns that suffered no destruction. A few families left for Syria, Jordan and the Lebanon, but this was for personal reasons rather than as refugees fleeing from a war zone. Today Sakhnin has about thirty thousand inhabitants, of which only about fifteen hundred are Christians, a mixture of Greek Orthodox and Greek Catholics. The rest are Muslims.

Kaukab, a much smaller village up in the hills between Sakhnin Valley and Beit Netofa, was engaged in fighting in 1948, with some people killed and several houses burnt and destroyed. A few families left for Jordan and Lebanon but eventually peace and quiet returned to the village. Kaukab has a population of only 2,800 and according to the locals it is 100% Muslim, with no influx from outside.

In the 1947 UN Partition, it was decided that the border between Israel and Palestine would run through the middle of the Christian village of Eilabun, at the eastern end of Beit Netofa Valley. When the British pulled out in 1948 and Israel declared independence, the Israeli army took the village. Local stories told to us described how the inhabitants fled to the church for safety, and that the Israelis shot some of the toughest looking men in order to make a strong impression, and then told the rest to leave. They fled to the Lebanon, and later negotiations between the Israelis and Church leaders secured their return. They returned six months later to find their property stolen, their crops burnt and many of their houses ruined. Today Eilabun is two thirds Christian, the Muslims being mostly Bedouin who have moved in during the past few decades. It is a quiet and peaceful village with a high percentage of well educated inhabitants.

In the upheavals during 1948, many Arabs from this area dispersed into Jordan and Lebanon. To this day, families are still looking for each other. In 2002 the authorities let people come right up to the Lebanese border to look for relatives, people they hadn't seen in fifty years, or had never met at all. People were shouting family names across the fence, in the hope of finding news of one another. Some of the refugees, who had left their homes over fifty years ago, were asking for news of villages that didn't even exist anymore.

Before modern local councils were introduced, the Mukhtars held the power in the villages and over the families or clans. According to the ex-mayor of Sakhnin, Jamal Tarabeah, these Mukhtars did not want high schools in the area. They were afraid of losing their power, which they thought would happen if people became better educated. Today this attitude has changed completely, and the Arab towns and villages in the Sakhnin Valley have a high proportion of university educated people.

Eilabun

Olive trees in the Sakhnin Valley

In 1963 the mayor of Sakhnin, Jamal Tarabeah, brought running water to the town, a big step forward for the inhabitants. Moshe Dayan, who was Minister of Agriculture at the time, called Jamal 'a rising star'. Eleven years later he introduced electricity. They needed a lot of money for this new lifestyle, but Jamal knew he could collect it from the residents of Sakhnin.

In 1976, the triangle of Deir Hana, Araba and Sakhnin saw the start of Yom ha Adama, or Land Day. The Israeli Army had changed the Sakhnin Valley from being an agricultural area to a firing range. There were demonstrations and strikes, and on March 30th the army came in with tanks to quell them, killing six young people. There is still no work done on that day and it is marked in different ways. Some see it as a public holiday, others hold demonstrations, some plant olive trees and some see it as a time for positive action towards mutual understanding and peace. Only in 1989 was the land returned to its original owners by Shimon Peres, and the army withdrew from the area.

During the 1980s the demography of the region changed drastically with the confiscation of common land on the hilltops around the valley. Many Jewish villages, including kibbutzim, were established, many of them with quite extensive land holdings. Even though most people realize that it is now impossible to turn back the clock, this aggravates the feeling of being hemmed in on all sides. Many of the people we talked to from Sakhnin and the surrounding Arab villages still resented the lack of building and public land available to them, while watching their Jewish neighbours expand their own villages and towns.

The situation once again became serious during the Second Intifada of October 2000 in Sakhnin and Araba. Apart from a few incidents, it was relatively quiet in Kaukab and the other villages. In one appalling incident police shot and killed a number of unarmed demonstrators and bystanders. The incident was made worse when a commission of enquiry found that no one in particular was to blame for the killings.

A few years ago the Sakhnin football team, Bnei Sakhnin (the sons of Sakhnin), won the championship in Israel. This catapulted Sakhnin into the headlines and was a tremendous boost for local self-esteem. The football stadium, on the road out of town leading to the Environmental Centre, is to this day a big attraction for football fans from all over the country. Many shops and cafes in the town display the red and white colours of the team, and have photos of the players on the wall.

Rather than doing research in a library, we asked everyone we interviewed to tell us about the history of the area. What you have now read is based on their stories. This may not be an objective historical account of the Valley of Sakhnin, but it is a reflection of how educated local people see their own personal background. As the local historian Rafeh Abu Raya commented, 'History is history; it only varies according to who tells it and when.'

Minaret and church tower, Muslims and Christians living side by side

Portrait of Jamal Tarabeah

Jamal Tarabeah

It came as quite a surprise to be sitting in Jamal's home, sipping spiced coffee from tiny cups, and hearing him quote Wordsworth and Byron in English to us. He wore a finely tailored suit and sat surrounded by his respectful family and admiring grandchildren — a grand, patriarchal figure. Jamal is an elderly, highly educated and distinguished Arab Muslim gentleman, equally at home with the Koran and classical English literature. He has been mayor of Sakhnin several times, and they could not have had a better representative.

Jamal finished high school in 1956 and began his career as a teacher. In 1968 he became mayor for the first time. Sakhnin was then a poor

Arab village, and he still feels that it was a major achievement to upgrade the village with new roads, water and electric power. For him, this was 'quality of the environment!' For the residents it was like a dream to have running water and electricity.

In the 1980s he wanted to be mayor again, with ambitions to improving Sakhnin even further, this time by installing a sewage system, which was completed in 1988. He was aware of the academic brilliance of one of the younger members of his extended family, Hussein Tarabeah, and together they worked on setting up the TAEQ.

More recently they have co-operated on a new theme, conflict resolution. Jamal is one of the elders of the town, recognized and accepted as someone who can help solve arguments between individuals and families. There is a strong tradition within the Arab world called *Sulha*, a method of reconciliation without recourse to violence. Jamal is still called out to help people, and Hussein is doing his postdoctoral research on conflict anticipation and resolution, using the *Sulha* as his starting point.

As we left, Jamal quoted from Mohammed the prophet, 'What is better than prayer and fasting? — To make peace between people.'

Portrait of Mustafa Abu Raya

Mustafa is a gentleman to his fingertips. At home he takes his jacket off, otherwise he is always dressed in a neat grey suit, even on the hottest days. He studied Chemistry and then Pharmacy at the Hebrew University in Jerusalem. He was a member of the Communist Party, very much believing in equality and co-existence between Arabs and Jews.

In 1989 he became mayor of Sakhnin and initiated many new ideas, including the beginnings of TAEQ with the help of Haim Shinhar and Yossi Sarid, the then Minister of the Environment. In Hussein Tarabeah he found just the right person to manage and develop the project.

After a few years Mustafa became tired of being mayor, and he wanted a new direction. That was when he went to study Banking and Business, for which he received a master's degree.

In 1998 Mustafa became mayor again. He brought in new, important improvements, such as psychological help in the health sector, an urban association, and better public services. He worked on Israeli,

Palestinian and Egyptian co-operation, which was much easier at that time. He believes fervently in the importance of Man's relationship to Nature, but even more, in Man's relationship to Man. He and Hussein travelled together to Egypt, and also to Istanbul for a conference on wastewater treatment. There were several exchanges between Turkey and Israel. Nowadays it's harder to organize and get Palestinians here, through the road blocks.

He is critical of Israel's treatment of her own Arabs. There is too much blatant inequality. 'Our demands are higher now, yet we receive less. They want to keep us small. We need to feel we belong. Let us join! I want to help this country to advance. Let me feel I belong and I will contribute …'

Mustafa Abu Raya

Hussein Tarabeah at his first office in the centre of Sakhnin, early 1990s

The first model of the site

2. Three Pioneers

In the 1990s I was working for the United Kibbutz Movement, encouraging and coordinating environmental projects. I met Hussein Tarabeah in the early 1990s through Life and Environment, an umbrella group of environmental organizations. He was the first Arab Israeli environmental activist that I had met, and he invited me to Sakhnin to see the project that he had described at the meeting. There wasn't much to see. A little office in the centre of the town, a cardboard model under a clear plastic cover, and some wastewater treatment ponds next to the town garbage dump. We drank coffee with the Bedouins who looked after the rubbish and Hussein gave me a short 'I have a dream' speech. I was impressed and we became friends. But of course the story of TAEQ began long before that moment.

First it was necessary for three men to meet.

In 1979, at the age of 35, Haim Shinhar left his kibbutz and his dairy cows and went to study at Haifa University. From there he went on to work for the National Parks Authority, then with the Nature Protection Society, and later moved over to the fledgling Department of the Environment, where he helped to set up the Northern Region Office. He had realized that the growing environmental awareness was all directed at the Jewish sector in Israel, and living as he did in rural Galilee he knew that a good deal of the region was dominated by Arabs and that they were 'way behind' in environmental issues. He knew standards had to be raised across the board and that, unless the Arabs were included, there could never be any large-scale improvement.

The garbage dump from where Hussein first showed me the present site of TAEQ

In the early 1990s Haim went to the Mayor of Sakhnin, Mustafa Abu Raya, and together they went to see Yossi Sarid, who was then Minister for the Environment. At this time Hussein was studying in Haifa and teaching Environmental Studies at high school level. It was the confluence of these three people that created TAEQ: Haim with his government contacts, Mayor Mustafa Abu Raya with his position in the town, and Hussein Tarabeah, the visionary environmentalist with the right academic qualifications. According to Hussein, when he first met Yossi Sarid in March 1993 it was not discussed *if* the office should be set up, but *when*. It was Yossi who came to cut the red ribbon! It was the first Arab Regional Environmental Quality Unit in the country and it was based on six of the surrounding towns and villages, with the central office in Sakhnin. The others were Araba, Deir Hana, Kaukab, Eilabun and Bu'neina-Nujeidat.

The office actually began on the ground floor of Said Khalaili's house, and then grew as meetings and courses proliferated. Enforcing new environmental laws was a big challenge in a society used to pretty much dumping rubbish indiscriminately. Haim told one story, about how he found a contractor dumping rubbish from Araba in Deir Hana, the next village down the road, instead of at the designated site a little further away.

Clearing some of the garbage away to make the site at the ponds, early 1990s

He and Hussein woke up the local mayor in the middle of the night to put things right. It was still early days, everyone was full of enthusiasm. They were pioneers, bringing environmental awareness to new fields.

Enthusiasm alone doesn't pay the bills and like many new organizations, TAEQ was struggling financially and coping with budget cuts. Sakhnin had just opened the new wastewater treatment plant on the eastern outskirts of the town and Hussein suggested creating an environmental project there. Haim thought this a brilliant idea. They were given three caravans by the Ministry of Education and that was the beginning of TAEQ as we see it today. There was no electricity, so they put in solar power. They began composting. They turned one of the caravans into a laboratory, others into classrooms. There were so many things to do besides just dealing with sewage. They went to visit alternative mud brick and straw bale buildings in Ma'alot, learning both new environmental and traditional methods of construction. They also made contacts abroad and got ideas for new projects.

The sewage pools at TAEQ are not in a suitable place. They are too close to the residents and block Sakhnin's development eastwards. People complain about the smell when the wind is blowing in the wrong direction. Hussein knew that this would cause conflicts with the locals because this area is agricultural land, so he thought it would be a positive step to convert the effluent into water for irrigation. We shall see later how this developed. The issue of the location of the site itself is still under discussion today and may lead to exciting new projects in the future.

Haim realized they had to find ways of bringing in money. This was the first regional environmental quality unit in the Arab sector, so there were few models for them to copy, and they had to encourage others to follow suit. Haim left office in 1997 but maintained his friendship and contact with Hussein. He carried on advising him on the office building, helping to turn it into an example of environmental retro-fitting. Mustafa Abu Raya has moved on from mayor, but he has also retained his connections with TAEQ, and it seems likely he will run the centre temporarily for a year while Hussein embarks on his post-doctorate research in the USA.

The official name of the unit is Towns Association for Environmental Quality, Agan Beit Netofa (TAEQ). Officially established in 1993,

The first classrooms on the site powered by solar panels

it gained status as a statutory body in 1996. It is not an NGO, being funded by the local municipalities and the Ministries of the Environment and the Interior. The Centre's projects can be divided into four main categories:

- Environmental education and awareness
- Sustainable environmental economic development
- Social projects
- Regional demonstration centre for wastewater treatment and irrigation

TAEQ is dedicated to increasing public awareness of environmental issues and increasing community involvement. To do this it works on such issues as water conservation, wastewater treatment, use of reclaimed effluents for agriculture, prevention of air and noise pollution, environmental planning, business licensing and recycling. The primary goals of the Centre include:

- Increasing awareness of the environment
- Protecting the environment

Composting toilets, solar panels and storage shed at the site, mid 1990s

- Future growth and economic development
- Organic agriculture
- Education and awareness
- Research and development
- Linking man to the land and environment
- Enforcing environmental laws in the community
- Establishing a regional centre for environmental education and technologies
- Providing assistance for professionals, farmers, teachers, and communities

In addition, TAEQ works with numerous schools and organizations to implement programs and projects that promote Jewish-Arab coexistence.

The wastewater treatment plant at TAEQ consists of a series of ponds starting with two parallel anaerobic (excluding oxygen) sedimentation ponds, each of which is 1,250 m^2 in area, and contains 5,000 m^3 of wastewater. There are two of these ponds, so one can be closed and emptied while the other is still in use, which needs to be done about once every five to seven years. The process taking place in these ponds is entirely natural. The oils and greases float to the top and create an airtight 'lid' which excludes oxygen and encourages the growth of natural anaerobic micro-organisms, that use the heavy pollutants in the wastewater as their nutrients. At the same time, solid matter settles on the bottom, gradually building up the layer that needs to be scooped out every few years.

After this about a third of the wastewater is piped off to Karmiel for further treatment, while the rest, today about 3,000 m^3 per day, goes to the oxygenation or facultative pond. This works in a rhythm based on diurnal (day and night) temperature differences, and the fact that warm water rises while cooler water sinks. The uppermost water layers take oxygen from the air and encourage an aerobic (including oxygen) process, not unlike what happens in a compost heap. Pollutants form nutrients for micro-organisms, in this pond both aerobic and anaerobic. This has the effect of removing a great deal more of the waste materials in the sewage. This pond is about the same size as the first two and retention time, the amount of time the wastewater stays in the pond, is two to three days in each of these three ponds. From here the wastewater is pumped into the much larger seasonal reservoir with a capacity of 150,000 m^3, and a retention time of several months, depending upon the season and the rainfall.

This system is known as an extensive system and is entirely natural, needs very little human intervention, but takes up a relatively large amount of space. The ponds at Sakhnin were the subject of a good deal of research during the early years, and detailed results were presented at an international workshop held at Agadir in Morocco in 1996 (see References).

The sewage from Sakhnin is mostly of a domestic nature, with human and food waste predominating. Since there is no heavy industry in the area of Sakhnin, toxins and heavy metals are not expected in the sewage in significant concentrations, and this is borne out by research. Coliforms and Streptococci form the most problematic pollutants, and these are significantly reduced during the treatment in the first ponds. After spending up to several months in the seasonal reservoir, the effluent is passed through a sand filter and then chlorinated, which brings it within the acceptable irrigation quality standards for olive plantations. Low chloride levels of less than 200 mg/L were found, permitting the irrigation of salinity-sensitive plantations such as almonds, citrus and avocado. A low rate of nitrification was found during the winter season while at the end of the summer season ammonia completely disappeared from the effluent. Total faecal coli form counts decreased by two orders of magnitude, and the count of faecal Streptococci decreased by a slightly higher degree.

To readers unfamiliar with further studies in Biology, this is basically good news. It means the effluent from the treatment plant can be used for irrigation of certain crops subject to controls. The solids that are emptied from the first two ponds every few years are mixed with shredded prunings and spread on the land as a compost or mulch. Small amounts of wastewater can be taken from any stage in the system and used for research purposes. Surplus wastewater, which the facility cannot handle, is pumped on to Karmiel to a much larger system there. For the thirty thousand people living in Sakhnin their sewage is taken care of, with only a slightly unpleasant odour at certain times. Certainly for us, living for half a year only a hundred metres away from the ponds, this was no problem, though we were aware of the smell from time to time.

However, the Centre is much more than just a place to clean sewage. It is used as a tool for education, it is a place for research, and for international co-operation. It was this aspect which excited us, and inspired me to write this book. How we can use sewage as a tool for co-operation and coexistence in this war torn region of the planet!

اتحاد مدن لجودة البيئة - حوض البطوف
مركز التثقيف والأبحاث البيئية
איגוד ערים לאיכות סביבה
אגן בית נטופה
המרכז לחינוך ומחקר סביבתי
TOWNS ASSOCIATION FOR ENVIRONMENTAL
QUALITY - AGAN BEIT NATUFA
CENTER FOR ENV. EDUCATION & RESEARCH

We were not the only ones to be inspired. Nearly every member of the TAEQ team that we talked to felt they were doing much more than just cleaning sewage. Bassem Ganaim is very involved with the LIFE Project, which we shall hear more about later, and that is what he's most proud of. He started about five years ago doing the groundwork for it, preparing the equipment. He fixes whatever needs fixing, but also helps the students with their projects, samples, tests and results. These are students doing research on projects for their final year at school.

Portrait of Hussein Tarabeah

Hussein maintains that the Muslim Arab Tarabeah family has been in Sakhnin for thousands of years, which would give them solid roots back amongst the Canaanites, with whatever religion they had, a spell as Second Temple Jews, a few centuries as Byzantine Christians, and nearly a millennia and a half as Muslims. This would give Hussein a good background from which to create bridges between the various religious groups now playing out their destiny in the Middle East.

In the late 1980s, Hussein was studying Biology at the University of Haifa under Professor Zelikson, and he became involved in a national project of the Israel Electricity Company (IEC) on fly ash, one of the by-products of generating electricity from burning coal. Greenpeace had caused a lot of problems for Israel because the country was dumping this solid waste in the sea. IEC had to find other solutions, and came up with the idea of dividing the ash between all the major cities in Israel. Hussein thought maybe they could grow certain bacteria that would leach poisons like cadmium and aluminium out of the fly ash, and maybe they could be reused. This was when he became interested in environmental issues. He was put in touch with Shlomo Kimchie to do this research. They met in Room 218 in the Borovitz Building and Shlomo agreed to be his tutor. It was to be a fateful meeting.

Previous pages:
Above left: Sand filter and chlorination unit in place in the mid-1990s, ready for irrigating the surrounding groves
Below left: The sign at the entrance to TAEQ in Arabic, Hebrew and English
Above right: The seasonal reservoir at TAEQ, with the town of Sakhnin in the background
Below right: The facultative or oxygenation pond

During the next three years the proposal to set up TAEQ was formulated in Sakhnin and the surrounding Arab towns. When Hussein was offered the job of managing TAEQ he was about to begin his PhD, but Shlomo advised him to go for the job. 'You can always do your doctorate later, in parallel with your job', he told him. It was only in 2008, a decade and a half later, that the PhD was finally finished.

Hussein is a man of his word, someone who turns dreams into reality. He is the protagonist on the stage. He is tall and imposing, and fits well into his role as manager of the Association. A pivotal figure, his mobile phone is constantly ringing and he is adept at juggling several conversations at once; people seem to be dangling at his fingertips. He has two large shiny tables in his spacious office, a computer and a laptop, and endless, but endless tiny cups of strong Arab coffee to keep the day's pace fast and animated.

Hussein Tarabeah

Haim Shinhar

Portrait of Haim Shinhar

Haim is like a tree trunk, planted firmly in the soil of the ecological village of Klil, further towards the coast from Sakhnin. He beams from ear to ear, eyes all a-twinkle, his face framed in his bushy, grey beard. He has a contagious enthusiasm and lots of *joie de vivre.* He inspires confidence by his very presence, you feel you can trust him implicitly, and when he speaks, he exudes a quiet authority. People listen to Haim. So much so that when the Ministry of the Environment began in the early 1990s, he quickly became head of the Northern Section. When he talks about Yossi Sarid, the first Environment Minister, he is clearly talking about a personal friend.

Haim was born and bred in Haifa, at a time when there were still small paths there, as yet no huge industrial complexes belching toxins into the beautiful bay. He had a fairytale childhood full of hiking, nature and animals. His German Jewish father had a close friend who was a biologist who had a great influence on Haim. To this day, he clearly remembers the pelican he had in his garden.

Haim studied Agriculture, specializing in dairy cow management, and despite having to take time out in the wars of 1967 and 1973, he worked as a dairyman in Kibbutz Giv'at Khayim. In 1979, at the age of 35, he left the kibbutz to study Geography and the Evolution of Religion, afterwards working his way through the National Parks Authority and into the newly started Ministry of the Environment. By this time he was living at Klil, and realized that the Arabs were vital to the environmental development of the Galilee. It was this realization that brought him into contact with Hussein Tarabeah and Mustafa Abu Raya, which eventually led to the founding of TAEQ.

TAEQ has four fathers — Yossi Sarid, Mustafa Abu Raya, Hussein Tarabeah and Haim Shinhar. Haim feels privileged to be one of them, and is honoured to have been given the opportunity to come closer to the Arab community.

3. Making an Impact

Hussein Tarabeah does not believe so much in talking as in doing. His method is not so much to persuade people, as rather to put things into action. So he built an access road, put in electricity, telephone connections and organized buses full of high school students to come to the Centre almost daily. People in Sakhnin began to sit up and see that something was going on. He wanted to show that sewage can be used for the benefit of the people in many different ways.

The years 1992 and 1993 were a turning point for Hussein. He could have carried on with his doctorate, but turned to the TAEQ project instead. This seemed to offer him a better future than just continuing with his doctorate, with possibly no great job prospects afterwards. However, he did continue with his studies in his spare time and in the spring of 2008, fifteen years later, he finally completed his PhD. By this time, TAEQ was well established as an internationally known and acclaimed environmental project.

It was clear to Hussein that the way forward for improving the environment was in the realm of education, not just inspecting local businesses and handing out fines. However, TAEQ itself had no educational budget. The Ministry of Education had been budgeting more and more money for environmental education during the early 1990s, encouraging schools to take it up to high school level (in Israel, the final examinations at high school level are called Bagrut, which is equivalent to university matriculation). In order to teach Environmental Studies at Bagrut level, schools have to invest heavily in laboratory equipment, research areas and teacher training. Hussein's experience as the first environmental teacher in the

Arab high school sector was enough to make him realize that a centralized facility serving several schools would be able to give high quality teaching at a fraction of the cost. The environment is a subject that cannot be taught frontally in the classroom, the students must come out of schools for activity and research.

This gave both Arab and Jewish schools in the Galilee wide options for school syllabus work, and training opportunities for students and their teachers. In turn this helped the Centre grow and advance, and in time to build up better equipment and resources. Other official bodies, like the Ministry of Health and the Ministry for the Environment, also became involved and were supportive. Once the Ministry of Education approved the proposed programme, the Centre received a budget and planning went ahead for a comprehensive environmental seminar centre. This development of environmental education, concentrating resources and saving schools money became the major financial driver for TAEQ. Today up to fifty thousand people visit TAEQ every year, the great majority high school students and their teachers. This creates employment for several people, and accounts for a large proportion of TAEQ's annual budget. Today 60% of those who study Environmental Studies in Israel at high school level are from the Arab sector.

Hussein also saw that he could use the Centre as a way of bringing together Arabs and Jews. In 1994 he participated in the Jordanian-Israeli Peace Agreement negotiations. He felt that environmental issues could become a bridge for peace, and that TAEQ could be a place for developing such ideas. He realized that without education and contact with the local community these kinds of projects could not succeed. He wanted this place to become an environmental centre for the entire region of the Middle East, and for all ethnic and religious groups. In 1998 Mustafa Abu Raya became mayor of Sakhnin again. The two of them travelled as part of a delegation to Egypt and Turkey. Mustafa worked on Israeli, Palestinian and Egyptian co-operation, which was more acceptable then than it is today in 2008. He believed in the importance of humankind's relationship to nature, but even more, in Man's relationship to Man. These trips resulted in several exchanges between Turkey and Israel on the subject of water usage.

These were ambitious ideas, and for them to succeed, Hussein realized that he would have to make an impact. Using the treated sewage

Above: Raw sewage killing olive trees in the Sakhnin valley
Below: Raw sewage and garbage in the olive groves near Sakhnin

for irrigation would be a major improvement for the local farmers, but it wasn't that simple. There was a psychological barrier to be overcome, as well as a *fatwa* imposed by the religious authorities. Using human sewage was taboo! In the Khula Valley, seventy kilometres to the north, there were Jewish farmers using treated wastewater and they provided the working example that the Sakhnin farmers needed. In order to make a start, they did not have to pay for their initial water usage. We shall see how this has developed further in Chapter 8.

The rural sector in Israel, the entire Middle East and North Africa has suffered from much neglect when it comes to wastewater treatment and reuse. The problem has become more acute in recent years due to the sharp increase in domestic water demand as the standard of living increases, and because of the continued water shortage. Lack of wastewater management has led to raw sewage flowing in the open, contaminating ground water and local wells which in turn have caused frequent outbreaks of water-borne diseases. Unauthorized irrigation has been the source of cholera outbreaks in some areas of the Middle East, leading to hospitalization and fatalities. News of such outbreaks also cause a reduction in tourism.

In the Mediterranean climate of the Middle East, with its long dry summers, there is an acute need for irrigation during those months, and storage of water to last the whole season. This requires open land for reservoirs not too far from the fields and orchards, and not too far from where people live, either. Some of the challenging conditions to be found in many communities in the region are: concentrated pollution of the wastewater due to relatively low total water use, high concentrations of pathogens, shortage of capital and availability of energy.

The motivation for investment in wastewater treatment plants can be increased by using the treated effluent for agricultural irrigation. This will add a financial incentive for increasing capital investments and paying for the expenses needed for proper operation and maintenance of the treatment facilities. Effluent quality can also be influenced by the decision to use these effluents for irrigation, while the treatment technology will be aimed at high standards of hygiene. By using the effluents for controlled irrigation much of the environmental risks caused by the other effluent disposal alternatives (for instance, disposal to rivers, lakes, sea, and so on) are prevented. From all this it is clear that both the farmers and the environment can benefit from effluent reuse in small communities.

Left: Raw sewage flowing alongside a road near Sakhnin

Portrait of Said Khalaili

Said Khalaili, standing, with two of the builders

Said Khalaili is one of the gentlest and friendliest men you will ever meet in Sakhnin, which is just as well, for he is probably one of the first you will meet at the Centre. He holds the place together on a day-to-day basis, his mobile phone constantly ringing with a catchy Arab tune. He answers the office phone, makes sure there is an endless stream of sweet hot coffee available, and can be seen constantly

on the move with his orange string of keys in one hand at the ready and always a wad of envelopes in the other. He fetches the post, visits the bank and the printers in town, and makes sure that everything is in place for meetings and seminars. He is always smiling and full of good humour.

He is proud to tell us that the Centre began its life in his house, renting a few rooms on the ground floor. Before that Said worked in an aluminium factory in Haifa. Most of his family is from Sakhnin, although his mother comes from Egypt.

He feels that the best thing he has done here was building the office complex using straw and mud bricks. He had no previous experience, but worked with the others at the Centre, making up to 150 bricks per day of different sizes with local earth.

Said Khalaili, in the grey shirt. Next to him is Yussuf Ganaim the night guard

4. Ecology and Coexistence

Wastewater treatment is not so difficult, given funding and willpower. All the technology is there. Education for high school students is similarly pretty straightforward. However, if there is one topic in the Middle East that is really complicated, it is the relationships between ethnic, political and religious groups like Jews and Muslims, Zionists and Palestinians, Lebanese, Jordanians and Israelis, to mention just a few.

Shlomo Kimchie is the only permanent Jewish member of staff at TAEQ, although from the beginning the intention has been for it to be a joint venture, one of dialogue and co-operation. Other Jewish Israelis, Haim Shinhar and Eitan Rozenberg, are connected to the Centre, contributing their expertise and advice.

When it comes to education, TAEQ has created involvement from both the Arab and Jewish sectors in Israel, with schools, teachers, youth leaders and students all combining projects and making connections. It has worked well, although admittedly it worked better before the events of October 2000, when the Second Intifada broke out and Israeli police shot a number of unarmed civilian Arabs, several in the immediate area of Araba. As Shlomo himself commented, 'If we do not work consciously in this direction, it simply will stop happening. It is much easier to destroy than to build …'

Hanadi Hijris, a Muslim Arab from the predominantly Christian village of Eilabun, doesn't feel that talking politics with the younger kids is the correct approach and is responsible for many of the educational programmes at TAEQ. She told me that 'both Arabs and Jews

have their own tragedies, and it is impossible to evaluate each other's feelings.' Therefore her approach is to try and find ways to work together for a common benefit, to accentuate the things that are in common, not the conflicts. She believes it's time to move forward in a positive manner. 'It's just not possible to take a computer and press the delete button on Israel; nor is it possible to delete the Palestinian people.'

One of the projects that Hanadi is passionate about is the Coexistence Project, something she shares with her colleague Khuzam Zriek, a Christian Arab, also originally from Eilabun. This project consists of bringing together Arab and Jewish teenagers from the region, from towns and villages such as Araba, Sakhnin, Tsviya and Rosh Pina. They discuss many issues, including cultural diversity, respect for each other's differences and the environment. They travel together and play together, and have now reached the stage where they can carry on their intercultural activities independently of the Centre. It is very difficult to assess what degree of success such activities can claim. Though lacking accurate, verifiable statistical data, I have a gut feeling that practically any activity which brings people together across the many and complicated fault lines of the Middle East must be a positive contribution in breaking down stereotypes and defusing violence, however small it might be.

Partnership for Peace (P4P) is a project which I can claim to know more about from my own involvement. In addition to the obstacles confronting Arabs and Jews, there is a need to build trust and understanding between Arabs living in Israel and those living in the Palestinian Authority in the West Bank and Gaza. I was asked to help teach a seminar for Palestinians, under the auspices of P4P and connected with the NGO, the 'Centre for Environmental Diplomacy' based in Ramallah in the Palestinian Authority. The aim was to teach a mixture of Permaculture environmental planning, organic agriculture and eco-tourism development. I had my doubts about the last topic, not really being able to envisage busloads of package holiday tourists negotiating roadblocks manned by heavily armoured Israeli soldiers. I just couldn't see how to market this as an attractive break for a European holidaymaker.

As it turned out we had over twenty participants, eighteen of them professional people from various towns in the Palestinian Authority, experts on agriculture, waste and water management, education and rural development. The Israeli participants numbered just four, all local Arabs active in environmental projects.

This is the front line. Here are minefields and rolls of barbed wire in every direction. What terms do you use? West Bank, Judea and Samaria, the Territories, Palestinian Authority? They all have heavy connotations and reveal your politics. What language do we use? Hebrew is a *lingua non grata* for many Palestinians, but often their English is not so good, and my Arabic is non-existent. Even alcohol is a dodgy subject; at one point I was illustrating a point about eco-tourism by talking about the development of small wineries in Israel when I realized I was way out there on very thin ice, the majority of the participants being Muslims, to whom alcohol is forbidden. No evening drinks in the bar with this crowd. We had arranged for the group to meet a wide number of people here in Galilee, all doing something related to the subjects we were covering. Several of these were Jewish. One comment we received from the feedback after the course was 'too many Jews'.

No one from the group wanted to be mentioned by name in this book, so the following comments I heard from various participants.

Their main problem is the occupation, and they felt the Israelis are not taking enough responsibility to talk peace. Programmes such as P4P create new relationships, but there can be no progress when Israelis insist on taking and keeping land that is not theirs. These programmes are too small, and despite good personal relations there is still no peace. Several of the Palestinian participants agreed that it's good to learn from Israelis, but that the Israelis should also learn from the Palestinians.

There is a serious problem with ground pollution in the Palestinian areas seeping into the water aquifers and polluting the water for everyone in the region, Jewish, Israeli, Palestinian alike. Geologically, the Palestinians are sitting on a limestone ridge overlooking the coastal plain. During the winter months, the relatively damp air coming in over the Mediterranean rises into the Judean mountains and cools, the humidity condensing out and falling as rain. This rain takes any ground pollution with it and filters down into the aquifer from which Israel pumps its water. According to the Palestinians I spoke with, there does not seem to be a great willingness on the part of the Israeli authorities to deal with this. The Israelis are the only ones that can grant licences for cleaning-up work to be done and for controlled garbage dumps to be set up, but they are extremely unwilling to do so. In this respect, the military occupation is actually harming Israel, threatening to destroy the viability of the aquifer upon which they depend for their water.

There are other problems of co-operation. Those wanting to attend these programmes have to apply for permission to leave the Palestinian Authority and obtain an entry permit into Israel proper, something which is often a problem. The Palestinian coordinator might have to submit twenty-five names in order to get fifteen licences. Sometimes they are all granted, and then the group is too big to handle. Sometimes individuals get an entry permit for the first workshop in a series of two, but not for the second. This creates a great deal of difficulty in continuity.

One of the speakers we brought in was Haggai Raban, a core person within the Israel Bio-Organic Agriculture Association, who talked about organic standards and how to attain them. He already works together with the Palestinian Agricultural Research Centre on the subject of organic standards, and during the discussion after his lecture it was mentioned that the Palestinians are cooperating with a Swiss organization, and with the Egyptian Organic Association. There are information bottlenecks, with an acute need for professional instructors and concentrated courses for local Palestinian farmers. Again we hit the political problem of the occupation, with exports being impossible to rely upon, due to Israeli blockades which can be imposed any time and easily lead to truckloads of fresh produce rotting while waiting at checkpoints in the Middle Eastern sunshine.

Partnership for Peace has been going as a project at TAEQ since 2007 and will run until 2009. It raises as many questions as it sets out to solve. It illustrates how far apart people are in the region, how suspicions and stereotypes are deeply embedded on each side of the many divides. But what else can ordinary people do? Politicians talk, but

Group of West Bank Palestinians on a visit to Sakhnin

Palestinians having a tour of a secondary school near Sakhnin

don't seem to get anywhere, the military on each side keep exchanging violence, and civilians keep getting hurt. Having been in and out of Israel for over thirty years, my experience is that fewer and fewer people I meet are optimistic about a peaceful solution. These brave attempts to do *something*, to get people together, need all the support they can get.

On safer ground, and with more optimistic prospects, was our meeting with LINK Foundation, an NGO active on environmental issues and Jewish-Arab dialogue and co-operation within Israel. It was set up in 1995, confining its activity to the Galilee area. Ahmad Hag is LINK's chairman and the former mayor of Kaukab. The managing director is Badria Biromi-Kandalaft, a Christian Arab, heavily pregnant when we met her, and currently living in Nazareth.

They listed some of the projects that they were engaged in, and were very happy co-operating on many of these with TAEQ. Two of their staff participated in a Permaculture Design Course that I was teaching, and personal friends of ours living in the area were active in one of the grass roots projects. Badria was a frequent visitor to the TAEQ office.

Projects developed by LINK included raising environmental awareness by pairing Jewish and Arab schools and initiating activities, cleaning trashed areas, developing community gardens and natural recreation spots, and helping general eco-tourism initiatives. They were working with about 150 garages in the area, recycling their used motor oil by linking them up with appropriate factories and industries, and had begun looking into bio diesel from used cooking oil as a means of replacing petrol. They were not afraid of getting involved in politics and were busy putting environmental issues on to the agenda of the local elections, due in November. At a real grass roots level, they had opened a second-hand shop in a local town, which was fast becoming a social centre with notice boards, talks and meetings.

The time spent and the budgets allocated for all these projects do not represent the major activity of TAEQ. Compared with the high school projects which we shall look at in the next chapter they are small fry indeed. But despite all the difficulties and the suspicions, they show that it is possible, and valuable, to bring people together to meet each other. A small budget, the equivalent of just one army tank or fighter aircraft, could be a really significant contribution to bringing peace to the region. The potential is there.

Portrait of Khuzam Zriek

Khuzam laughs easily but her happy, open demeanour and European style of dress belie her traditional background.

She never expected to end up in charge of the laboratory and the library at TAEQ. At the end of the 1990s she took part in a competition, and won a grant to study Environmental Science at the Technion in Haifa. She applied on the very last day, got a place, and in her second year, Hussein Tarabeah was one of her teachers. Through this contact she became one of the guides at the Centre for a while. Then she went to do a project for six months at the Alternative Planning Centre in her home town of Eilabun, where she worked on planning maps of environmental pollution in the local area. She came back to guiding at TAEQ and finished her studies when she had saved enough money.

From guiding she began working in the laboratory, analyzing samples on her own, and was later joined by a student from Istanbul University. She feels that her greatest success working here has been her involvement in the LIFE Project, taking sets of results and breaking them down scientifically.

She has also worked on the Coexistence Project with young Arab and Jewish school kids. Sometimes there are groups that everybody has a problem working with, but with perseverance she is able to get through to them. She commented, 'You really have to want to do this work, like the kids and understand them.'

Khuzam Zriek in her laboratory

High school students doing fieldwork at TAEQ

5. Educational Projects

'Well, the whole place is an educational centre,' said Mukhles Hajouj, who creates new educational programmes every year. He agrees that the aims of dialogue and co-operation covered in the previous chapter are vitally important, and is actively using environmental education as a leverage tool for co-operation and connection between Jews and Arabs. He quoted the by now familiar phrase, 'the environment knows no borders!'

High school students are his main concern, for whom he creates environmental workshops, where students take on various environmental projects. They must complete certain assignments, ongoing projects throughout the year, for which they then receive credits that contribute towards their Bagrut matriculation.

TAEQ has been active in supporting students by providing topics for credit-earning school projects in a variety of fields. It is important for the Arab community to take an active role in addressing its own issues by self-education and self-help. Mukhles helps young Arabs be proactive in preserving their environment. He and his group of guides conduct daily tours and give opportunities for schools and other visitors to see the facilities and view first hand the methods of environmental protection and development that are taught here. These programmes often involve parents and start at kindergarten level, making herb gardens, benches and statues. There are tours for older school pupils from the area, and programmes for high school pupils in both Biology and Environmental Studies, leading to university entrance exams. The aim is to raise environmental consciousness throughout the area in the local villages and towns.

The water treatment plant itself has laboratories and classrooms, and the Centre has an environmental library, all of which are accessible to local communities. Students and teachers from all the local schools and high schools can participate in study days, using the field laboratories to gain hands-on experience of advanced scientific equipment, develop analysis skills, and study different environmental projects. The Centre serves as a resource for professional workers in the agricultural and environmental protection fields. The training programmes also affect local decision makers in the areas of environmental protection, agriculture, and energy.

The Centre is continually examining new methods, upgrading and experimenting, in order to increase the efficiency, quality, and quantity of the effluent. The construction of wetlands in the wastewater treatment process and experimentation with a variety of flora are examples of this development, as are the experiments to develop a natural method to heat one of the anaerobic ponds. Another priority is to make the Centre self-sufficient in energy use.

Over the years, many smaller projects have been followed up here. They established a nursery for decorative trees that used reclaimed wastewater to irrigate the saplings.

They organized a seminar on the subject of wastewater management in the Middle East. They prepared a learning programme for Jewish and Arab high school students from Acre and Sakhnin. The programme was based on research on the subject of stream pollution. They organized a course for teachers who guide high school students, preparing teaching material in both Arabic and Hebrew. They created an environmental mission statement for local mayors to sign. They initiated courses for nurses in environmental studies with support from the health department. They began plastic bottle recycling, but found that plastic bottles were being used to store pickled olives, so discontinued working with a contractor for recycling, preferring to encourage reuse of the bottles instead.

Probably the single biggest educational project TAEQ has undertaken is Green Net Schools. This has been running since 2002 and is aimed at teachers of 10-16 year olds. There are many schools from all over the country involved in this project, sixty Arab schools, including five from Sakhnin, and sixty-three Jewish schools.

The project is aimed at helping teachers to build up environmental programmes. Each programme is individually tailored to suit the particular needs of the school. The basic pattern is to start in the classroom, beginning with the individual and working outwards towards the school, village, community and the environment at large. In this way, the pupils learn to know themselves better, and eventually make improvements and changes that are appropriate. They learn how to look and enjoy and appreciate, and have a lot of choice in their activities. Hanadi, who is very involved in this project, told us about one group who were not so interested in talking about the environment. They wanted to dance! So this was facilitated — first they danced, learning about local traditional dance, and from there moved on to clothes and lifestyle, connecting their lifestyle to their local environment.

At the end of each project the community is invited into the schools to see all the topics presented, and to get involved in them further. Each year, in addition to many different environmental topics, there is one particular theme common to all. In 2008, the theme was community, the idea being that a strong community has more power.

As part of the P4P programme for Palestinians, I joined a tour of the high school in the nearby Arab village of Rama. This is one of the schools that TAEQ works closely with, and as the tour was in Arabic, and my translator was one of the Palestinian participants, I got some interesting perspectives on the school.

We were taken round by Abed Al Majed who explained that the school takes Arab students from the surrounding villages in the region, up to Bagrut level. Amongst other subjects it offers Agriculture as a separate line, including some organic agriculture theory. He explained that political decisions in Israel give teachers and schools a very low status, low salaries for teachers and low budgets for schools. Rama School had old, outdated equipment and buildings, and only government approved contractors can carry out government funded building projects. These contractors are usually up to four times as expensive as local contractors. Education in Israel has been devalued over the past years, and both Jewish and Arab sectors are threatened by this. It is also generally accepted, and unfortunately not contested enough, that the Arab sector is often under-budgeted as compared to the Jewish. So a school like Rama suffers twice over. Interestingly enough, my Palestinian interpreter commented that schools within the Palestinian Authority compare favourably to the Rama school.

Rama school twins with a school in Germany, a contact that was initiated by Abed Al Majed, who studied in Germany. The German school has contributed a snack bar, a very handsome round building with a beautiful wooden-framed roof, in addition to various pieces of educational equipment.

The school only has 50 dunam of land to work on, and there are complicated demands made of them as to how to use it. They do not grow organically, but there is a proposal to turn part of it into an organic training farm. The motivation is that there is a great deal of organic farming locally, especially in the growing of olives, and so it would be more appropriate to the area. Another reason is that Abed sees a general trend towards organic growing, and a steadily increasing demand for organic produce, and that this sector is expected to expand. According to him, there is no support from the Ministry of Education to switch to organic methods. Low salary and general lack

Ancient olive tree near Deir Hana, sporting four trunks growing from the same root

of prospects in agricultural professions lead to low priority for agricultural training. Throughout Israel, only two schools in the Arab sector offer agricultural training, as compared to thirty-five Jewish schools.

Abed Al Majed comes from Deir Hana, where he also farms organic olives. His immediate neighbours have trees that are marked on Israeli maps as 'old olive trees'. How old is hard to know. One expert said that it was virtually impossible to be certain, as regrowth from old root stocks makes ring counting useless. Many trees are claimed to be anything from one to four thousand years old. The expert, when pressed, shrugged and answered 'could be'.

Abed's organic management shows that low input management, with no use of chemicals or artificial fertilizer, pays off. The only input is work, ploughing once a year, some hand weed-pulling, harvesting and pruning. Pruning is the most important task in order to increase yields. No watering is needed.

As the environmental crisis tightens its grip on the countries of the Middle East, it could be that growing food and cultivating the soil will again become vitally important subjects to be taught and learnt. Certainly TAEQ will be way ahead of the game.

Portrait of Mukhles Hajouj

Talking to Mukhles is like being in the midst of a hurricane. He is full of quivering energy, able to hold several conversations, answer his mobile phone and scroll on his computer screen, all at the same time. A Muslim Arab from Kaukab, he is short and compact, sleeves rolled up ready for work, in many ways holding the Centre together by keeping tabs on everyone's appointment diaries.

He studied Environmental Engineering, and worked for ten years in education, in Beer Sheba down in the Negev, and locally in Tamra and Araba. He still lives in Kaukab, where he is involved in the local council and in projects to do with culture and education.

He is in charge of all the groups that come to the Centre, both their educational programmes and their budgets. The list of his responsibilities is both long and exacting: requests for grants, budgeting, contact with schools and councils, other educational establishments and environmental groups, extra-curricular activities, youth leadership programmes, contact with the Technion and Haifa University. In addition, he helps local councils apply for money from the state for environmental projects such as local clean-up campaigns. He is also involved with Brit Chinuch Lstudentim — a student educational organization.

He joined the staff at TAEQ in 2000, becoming involved in this particular project because Hussein Tarabeah was one of his teachers.

He is hard to pin down for a meeting, his agenda changes by the minute, and even in meetings he is often busy talking to others on his mobile phone. But sometimes there is a lull in the storm, and if you can catch him then he talks enthusiastically about the house he is building for his family, and the football matches at Sakhnin which he attends regularly and loyally.

Mukhles Hajouj

6. Permaculture Complications

When the opportunity to come to Sakhnin arose for me, Hussein's first comment was, 'Wonderful, now we can work together at the Centre, and you can do Permaculture!' Well, life wasn't that simple.

Permaculture is about designing sustainable human settlements. It is a philosophical and practical approach to land use, integrating microclimate, functional plants, animals, soils, water management and human needs into intricately connected, highly productive systems. Permaculture means thinking carefully about our environment, our use of resources and how we supply our needs. It aims to create systems that will sustain not only for the present, but also for future generations. The idea is one of co-operation with nature and each other, of caring for the earth and its people.

Permaculture began in the mid 1970s when Bill Mollison was teaching Ecology at the University of Tasmania. He formulated the idea together with one of his students, David Holmgren. It was then thought of as an interdisciplinary earth science with a potential for global outreach. The first book, *Permaculture One*, was published in 1978, and the first Permaculture Design Course (PDC) was taught in January 1981. By this time the concept was already sweeping across the western alternative world, and Permaculture groups were gathering in many places.

Mollison called Permaculture 'a complete agricultural ecosystem' and 'a pioneer effort in perennial agriculture' in the introduction to *Permaculture One*. He goes on to say that it was initially aimed at small groups, living on cheaply available, marginal land. Within a couple of decades, Permaculture had developed from a better way of farming and gardening, to a design tool which could be applied to virtually any human situation. By adapting to widely different ecosystems, Permaculture became a set of principles rather than a recipe.

Permaculture looks for the patterns embedded in our natural world as inspirations for design solutions to the many challenges we are presented with today. It encourages individuals to be resourceful and self-reliant and to become a conscious part in solving the many problems which face us both locally and globally.

My first involvement with TAEQ was actually giving short seminars on Permaculture together with other Permaculture instructors to the staff there in the mid-1990s. The word caught on, but I don't think that the idea was understood so well. It was still early days, it was hard to put it across in Hebrew, and there were cultural differences. The Arabs in the Sakhnin Valley had different agendas from us eco-activists.

A year ago, TAEQ received a grant to run a series of Permaculture Foundation Courses, known as the PDC — a seventy-two-hour standard curriculum, recognized throughout the world. One of the aims was to create another meeting place, a contact zone, between Arabs and Jews. This was not so easy. The first course had only three Arabs, as opposed to twenty-five Jewish participants, the second course was exclusively Jewish, and the third course, which I taught, had an all-time high of seven Arabs starting the course, but only four actually completing. Of all the participants, only two part-time staff of TAEQ participated. TAEQ was acting as a host seminar centre, but was not itself participating in the seminars. The place was doing Permaculture by hosting courses, not really doing Permaculture by looking at how much thought was going into presenting working compost systems, reusing paper, recycling its own wastes or rainwater harvesting. Some of the Permaculture instructors who had taught at Sakhnin felt that the staff were lacking interest in implementing Permaculture as anything more than another educational product. In the fast-expanding world of Israeli Permaculture, TAEQ was not exactly a star.

There are great cultural differences that operate here, which makes it very difficult to translate the kind of Permaculture teaching I had developed into something understandable to the Israeli Arab world. Sakhnin is well within the borders of Israel, all its residents are citizens of Israel, they pay taxes, and are cared for by the education, health and social security systems. It astounded us how many ordinary Israelis we encountered who thought that Sakhnin was in the Palestinian Authority (the West Bank occupied territories) or that it was somehow a foreign land. 'Do they speak Hebrew? Can you walk around the town? What are they *really* like?' We got used to all these questions, and had our answers ready, but try and imagine that you are the one being asked about. What kind of self-esteem does this create? How does this affect your agenda?

Permaculture is a response to bad environmental management. It's a kind of protest movement, albeit focussing on creating good ecological design. For an Israeli Arab, protest against the standing order may not be high on the agenda. Being seen, being accepted, becoming part of the mainstream may be more important. The percentage of people going through higher education seemed to me very high in the Arab villages around us. Suits and ties were common, unfamiliar attire for most Jewish Israelis. The symbols of success were all around us, grandiose houses, flashy modern cars, multiple mobile phones ringing all the time. Most Permaculture teachers and designers I know in Western Europe have no time for this. They want to create an alternative. Before many of the Israeli Arabs want to create an alternative, I believe they want a slice of the cake. They have a different agenda.

No, introducing Permaculture to TAEQ was not so simple, but I didn't give up.

Teaching Permaculture is very different from teaching Environmental Studies in schools. It focuses more on the individual and how to alert each person to take responsibility for the environmental consequence of their lifestyles and decisions. Permaculture teaches that you start small, and in a busy work situation it is often the small things that get neglected. So at the Centre we were involved in making contact with fifty thousand people a year on the subject of environmental awareness and action, and yet we were using plastic cups in large quantities. There were no rainwater harvesting schemes, and seemingly no awareness of this as a subject or a reality.

One of the Permaculture instructors working here said it in this way, 'This place lacks a soul'. Well, in one way he was right. No one lives here, it's a place of work, where people clock in every morning stamping a time card, and are, like most normal people, eager to get home to their families in the evening. The instructor I talked to was concerned with the unrealized potential of a large seminar centre which could be a community centre, open sixteen hours a day and offering a wide variety of groups an even wider variety of activities.

As a Permaculture instructor he was well aware of the principle that in any well-planned system, one element should provide many functions. TAEQ could include a club for geriatrics, a café, a cinema, a vegetable growing club, a workshop for handicrafts, a park, and a petting zoo. The only limit is the imagination.

Hanadi had taken a Permaculture course a few years ago, run by Talia Schneider, one of the leading Permaculture instructors in Israel. Inspired by this, her own ideas, and a low budget kindergarten in Holland that she had visited, Hanadi decided to go to work on Sakhnin. Her aims were minimal expenditure and maximum enjoyment in a small area, using environmental consciousness. For a couple of years she focussed on kindergartens in the town, and while we were staying she took us on a tour.

She maintains that it's easier to build correct behaviour and attitudes to the environment at an early age. With this in mind, she set up a course for the kindergarten teachers on environmental issues. Each teacher then has an ongoing guide or adviser to help them create a programme to incorporate these issues into their syllabus.

Hanadi faces a serious infrastructure problem when working with kindergartens in that there are no public play areas or municipally owned kindergartens in Sakhnin. They are always located in the yard or the cellar of people's private houses, but they learn to beautify their simple surroundings by decorating the walls and growing plants. Because they are not purpose built it is a major challenge to turn them into attractive, inviting places for kids to grow and flourish, and to use the space in the most economical way possible. Each kindergarten we visited had very limited space, around 38 children, and only two or three staff. Parents pay only 250 shekels a year, and the kindergartens and salaries are supported by the Ministry of Education.

The first kindergarten we visited was like stepping into a surprising, colourful, safe, beautiful and exciting child's world. Off a dilapidated, grey, concrete street, the entrance was a burst of colourful flowers in a miniature rock garden, shaded by fresh green vines, water cascading down a rocky wall into a pool, providing water for a sheltered herb garden planted in old tyres. Pretty mobiles made of plastic bottles hung everywhere. Parental involvement was encouraged for help with building, decorating and gardening. Inside, the kindergarten was very

Above: Permaculture Design Course group doing field work at TAEQ
Below: Kindergarten forecourt in Sakhnin

reminiscent of any modern, western kindergarten, remarkable considering their limited resources.

The second kindergarten also had a happy welcoming atmosphere. Although there was slightly less to see here of Hanadi's influence, she explained to us that what was most impressive about this particular kindergarten, was their 'outreach' work. The children take their new-found knowledge and ideas out into the community. For example, they make regular visits to the old age homes to teach the residents (many of whom are illiterate) what they have learnt, numbers, and letters of the alphabet. The outside yard was full of painted tyres and homemade climbing equipment and had a special corner for storytelling.

At the third kindergarten we saw use of simple materials for impressive and beautiful results. Here a hessian sack to decorate a metal staircase, there a mural of a traditional Arab scene painted by a local artist. Inside the kindergarten there was a quiet blue corner to calm the hyperactive. Little bottles filled with coloured plastic bags, or layers of beans and lentils. A handmade memory game of prettily painted stones, stored with care in an old egg carton.

And outside, here was the empty, concrete, sun-blinding yard and Hanadi's sad story of how one night the owner had flattened their many months of hard labour, a labour of love, of planting fruit trees, herbs and flowers in Permaculture style. He needed the space for his son's wedding party. Afterwards he somewhat regretted what he had done, and understood that for one evening's private enjoyment, he had destroyed many years of children's learning, love and respect for nature and the environment.

So to introduce Permaculture to Sakhnin and to the Centre is a challenge. It's an unfinished story, meetings are still going on, plans are being introduced, and the outcome is not known. One thing that is certain is that it will not be the Permaculture that is familiar to us from Western Europe, from Australia or North America. And that is how it should be. Permaculture needs to adapt to specific local conditions, and hopefully that is what will happen here too.

Kindergarten entrance in Sakhnin

Portrait of Eitan Rozenberg

Eitan is a busy man, with many projects going on at the same time. Tall and good looking, he exudes quiet energy and confidence. Competent and powerful, he is clearly used to telling people what to do, but still able to listen to their ideas and incorporate them into the project in hand. It came as no surprise to hear that he is a captain in the Israeli Navy reserves.

Born and bred in Tel Aviv, he studied Agriculture after finishing the navy, but found university life too theoretical and left to pursue one of his dreams, keeping bees, a hobby he still continues to this day.

By chance, he was offered a job by the Herzliya Municipality inspecting the city's gardens, and making sure the garden contractors were actually carrying out the jobs they were hired to do. This was the first local government job of this kind in Israel, and he did ground-breaking work, defining the appointment.

Eitan Rozenberg surrounded by Permaculture students

During the 1980s Israel was encouraging Jewish settlement in the Galilee, and Eitan joined a group that eventually built up the village of Tzviya, a few kilometres from Sakhnin. He and his wife arrived with their nine month old baby to live in a caravan on the site, and with no job. He bought a van and went into the gardening business. After only a few months he was offered a job by the Misgav local authority as landscape advisor, a post he held for seventeen years, which brought him into contact with many people in the area.

In 1996 he participated in a Permaculture course and now, twelve years later, he is co-teaching his third Permaculture Design Course. Contact with TAEQ didn't come until 2003, again through a chance connection, and in the last few years he has undertaken many planning projects for them. Currently he is in charge of the landscaping around the Green Building, and a major project turning the sewage-filled marshes near Araba into a people's park with clean lakes and recreational areas.

Eitan Rozenberg explaining drainage systems to Permaculture students

Portrait of Hanadi Hijris

Hanadi heard about TAEQ from Hussein when he was her teacher in Ecology and the Environment. She had trained as a teacher and asked him to be her supervisor when she had teaching practice. When he heard her give a lecture on the beaching of dolphins, he invited her to come and work at the Centre.

She visited and it was the closest thing to her dream, even though at the time there was very little to see. She imagined this beautiful place, full of animals and plants, students and even a farm. Maybe here she could 'touch' her dream ...

She started as a guide for the students in 2001, but soon realized she would have much more potential as one of the team preparing educational programmes. Hanadi has been a full-time member of staff since 2003, with responsibility for programmes such as Partnership for Peace, the Coexistence Project and Environmental Leadership in Sustainable Development.

One or two trinkets adorn her small office, colourful examples of her fine workshops with Arab kindergarten teachers — a simple mobile made of nature's bounties, a painted pinecone, a beautifully decorated stone.

Her Muslim family is from Eilabun, and she did her BSc degree at Oranim, a department of Haifa University, where she specialized in Zoology and Marine Ecology.

I can't help noticing the gold pendant around her neck — a miniature Israel with the Palestinian flag stretching right across it. Behind her desk, a sombre poster, also a map of Israel with the slogan, 'We will return'. However, she doesn't feel that talking politics is the correct approach to attaining reconciliation. Both Arabs and Jews have suffered their own tragedies, and it is impossible to evaluate each other's feelings. Therefore her approach is to try to find ways to work together for a common benefit, to accentuate the things that are in common, not the conflicts. She really believes in Arab-Israeli co-operation.

Hanadi is full of smiles and easy laughter. She exudes self-confidence and speaks openly in fluent Hebrew, like the rest of the staff, but also in good English. She has travelled several times to Europe, is proud of her Arab heritage yet Western in her style of being.

Above: Hanadi, relaxing with friends
Below: Hanadi, in sunglasses, talking to a Palestinian delegate

7. LIFE in the Sewage

TAEQ was the first research and demonstration centre of its kind in the Arab sector in Israel. The Centre is a pilot project that can be used as an example for other communities in this region facing the problem of scarce water resources. The system itself is based on natural processes for wastewater treatment and is simple and reliable with relatively low expenses. In addition, it is uncomplicated and doesn't need a great deal of technical, expensive maintenance. It has a low environmental impact. All of these factors and its easy replication make it the most appropriate wastewater treatment system for the region.

Community education about the fragility of the environment and various issues that affect it is extremely important. Education is the real long-term strategy to develop public awareness regarding the use of water and wastewater in rural communities. As we have seen in previous chapters, education plays a central role in TAEQ.

High school students, preparing for their Bagrut, need to combine learning with research, and one of the big achievements of TAEQ was the LIFE Project. This is funded through the European Union and is a large research project, aimed at developing better wastewater treatment processes. The project took the most primitive, cheapest and simplest system for dealing with wastewater, and started work on improving it as much as possible. They began with the poorest quality water, which produces gases of the kind that cause global warming. They experimented with burning these gases and producing energy. Other experiments consisted of heating the wastewater, or diluting it, finding out how to adapt the system to optimum conditions. They have experimented successfully with putting different prunings in the water, where the prunings not only disintegrate, but also destroy certain pathogens. They have also experimented with constructed wetlands, where they have tried combining different kinds of stones and plants. There are eighteen experimental projects, all with different strategies to prevent environmental problems.

The project expanded, not least because those involved felt proud to be part of it. Khuzam Zriek began working in the laboratory, doing analyses on her own, and was later joined temporarily by a student from Istanbul University. She told us proudly of the praise she had received for her reports. Jummana Essa considers LIFE to be her main project, and the one of which she is most proud. She commented, 'This was the first large grant we received at the Centre, and the first major project. Now we have the infrastructure in place for future use.'

Research activities designed to help develop rural areas became a separate department within TAEQ. The Sakhnin Rural Development Centre (SRDC) came to include such facilities as laboratories, classrooms, a lecture hall, office services, pilot plant experimental units, field experimental equipment and a computerized meteorological station. The SRDC is part of TAEQ and operates in the areas of education, research and development with environmental, agricultural and energy issues as the major fields of interest. The fact that the TAEQ and SRDC facilities are located next to the wastewater treatment plant demonstrates that a well-maintained plant can be operated in rural areas without inhibiting educational and other activities. Research which can help upgrade existing technology serves as 'leading subjects' for about ten research projects per year for high school and college students.

There are many educational activities carried out by the SRDC, including work with elementary schools, high schools, academic institutions, and adult professionals such as teachers, engineers and planners. These educational activities include study days, workshops, and environmental tours of the centre. About eighty projects per year are led by instructors on chemical, environmental, and agricultural subjects related to wastewater treatment and effluent reuse. This educational activity also includes annual workshops on related subjects. These workshops are excellent opportunities for students to present

Above: Shlomo at one of the LIFE Project experiments
Below: Part of the LIFE experiment site

TASK 1.4 - Constructed Wetlands
משימה 1.4 - אגנים ירוקים
مهمة 1.4 - أحواض خضراء

R-5
R-6
TASK 1.4 - Constructed Wetlands
משימה 1.4 - אגנים ירוקים
مهمة 1.4 - أحواض خضراء

their work, and for others to listen and acquire a deeper understanding on various topics dealing with environmental engineering. The LIFE project also involves bi-national and international exchanges, a topic we shall look at in further detail in Chapter 10.

It is this last aspect which keeps Jummana busy. She is continually looking for grants from new foundations and making contacts with donors. Not only is TAEQ helping Sakhnin deal with its sewage in a useful and responsible manner, but it is using the subject as a way of creating international ties across continents. The effluents from all the treatment stages of the Sakhnin plant serve as raw materials for this research.

At all stages, the effluent is monitored to ensure that the chemical content of the effluent is correct. The removal of dangerous wastes occurs in various stages, with the transfer of the wastewater between the different pools. The creation of wetlands and the filtration sections of the project ensure the highest quality of reusable water.

Portrait of Jummana Essa

Jummana was born into a Greek Catholic Arab family in Alabama and raised in South Carolina, USA. Her father had left Eilabun to study Political Science in the USA, and her mother became a preschool teacher there. Jummana speaks English with a strong southern drawl. She grew up speaking Arabic at home, but finds it difficult to read or write it.

Jummana's roots were strong and powerful, in fact strong enough to pull her all the way back from the States to the small, unpretentious and unremarkable Arab town of her ancestors. Both her parents are from Eilabun, and she moved back to her family town in 2002, after first completing a degree in Health and Exercise Science, and then a Master's in Public Health. In between raising her children and her job at TAEQ, she is doing a PhD in Haifa on Internet-based Health Education.

She moved back initially just for six months, but liked it so much she ended up staying, getting married and having twins. Her husband studied journalism at Tel Aviv University. She started work at TAEQ in 2002, where she is responsible for international relations, writing grant proposals and reports, in fact anything that needs writing in English.

Her biggest challenge here is the cultural difference. Things are left till the absolute last minute for deadlines, which sometimes means that opportunities are missed.

Jummana Essa

8. Local Farming Initiatives

The agriculture that has been developed over the last half century or more, which insists on using large amounts of industrial chemicals and oil-based heavy technology, has created more problems than it has solved. Many people may not agree with my opinion on this, but the fact is that the number of those who support organic and biodynamic farming increases relentlessly year after year, as does the number of those starving which modern industrial farming fails to feed. Officially TAEQ also shares my view of agriculture, though we did notice that a commitment to support organic farming through buying its products was not strongly in evidence amongst the staff. However, it is difficult to obtain certified organic food in Sakhnin.

For one of our seminars we had invited Haggai Raban of the Israel Bio-Organic Agriculture Association, as previously mentioned in Chapter 4. He opened his presentation by showing how organic, biological, biodynamic and ecological agriculture was expanding all over the world. He carried on by explaining how there was a need for protection of the customer, who trusts that he or she will get organic when buying it. This is the area of quality control, or in other words, organic standards and their enforcement. As we saw in Chapter 5, TAEQ works together with schools which favour organic agriculture. There is no doubt the Centre is actively seeking partners sympathetic to a switch from chemical/industrial farming to organic.

Above: National Water Carrier in Beit Netofa Valley
Below: Beit Netofa Valley with the National Water Carrier cutting straight through it

TAEQ's link with the local farmer is through the use of treated effluent for irrigation. As we shall see, this is still quite small-scale. The other link is through the planning processes, especially when it comes to land use and development. Here TAEQ has become very engaged, but it's an area which is not without problems and conflicts.

In March, I attended an open meeting at the Centre, where local farmers had been invited, along with residents of all the villages, Jewish and Arab, that fringe the Sakhnin Valley, together with representatives from organizations that supported Jewish-Arab co-operation. A planning group had been working on a general zoning and development plan for the whole valley, designed to encourage organic growers, eco-tourism and the development of small-scale local enterprises which would impact minimally upon the environment. The plan was also designed to clean up damaged land.

It was clear that a great deal of importance was given to co-operation between Arab towns and the Jewish villages in the area. The development of eco-tourism and agriculture was high priority. It was a complicated situation involving several national bodies: the Department of Agriculture, the Jewish National Fund and the National Parks Authority among them. The underlying reasons for the project were clear. There is a lack of public parks in Arab towns and villages, and generally a need for recreation areas. There is also a need to increase sources of income for the rising population in all the towns and villages in the valley. Some of the suggested solutions incorporated organic and traditional agriculture attractive for tourists, and developing water features such as streams, ponds and lakes. Bird watching could also be important and attractive.

The meeting was stormy. There was a lot of shouting and arguing. Even though the plan was presented as a suggested starting point of a process, and participants were invited to take part in future planning meetings, it was received as an attempt to coerce residents into something they didn't want. It was difficult for me to understand what was going on.

One local person we talked to commented that he does not support this project because it will endanger the Arab farmers. He saw the plan as an excuse for the state to gain more land. He supported converting the valley to organic agriculture, for both Jews and Arabs, on an equal basis, but maintained that there is no equality between the communities at the present time. He was not prepared to trust government policy or the municipalities, only the good of the people. Personally I found it hard to relate his criticisms to the plan that was presented.

Was this just the generally argumentative Middle Eastern way of carrying on open discussions? Were there hidden agendas, a previous history of conflicts carried over from the past? Was this another culture clash, between the traditional paternal, hierarchical power pattern, and the new, western pattern of flat democracy?

The neighbouring valley of Beit Netofa is also the subject of stormy debate. It is owned by Arabs from the surrounding villages, including Sakhnin, and covers about 40,000 dunam. Some land was taken by Israel in order to build the National Water Carrier (NWC) in 1964, in order to bring water from the Sea of Galilee down to the Negev Desert. Along most of its route the NWC is in a closed pipe, but across Beit Netofa it is open, taking up a great deal of agricultural land. The water is not made available to local farmers, but they see the water flowing past their fields every day. The canal makes movement difficult because there are few bridges. The NWC was licensed to take 100 dunam for the canal, but took 1,500, and the farmers maintain that they still have not received compensation. The canal also disturbed the natural movement of water in the valley, and the authorities will not issue licences for private water harvesting and storage. This was how the local farmers saw the situation.

Beit Netofa valley with the National Water Carrier cutting through the middle of the farmland

During the winter rains Beit Netofa Valley often floods, and this has become a national attraction when viewed from the hills around. Someone called it a fjord, but as a Norwegian I felt this was stretching a point. There is no doubt, though, that the lake in winter is good for tourism, but this does not benefit the farmers in the valley very much. Summer irrigation would change the environment, which might be good for the farmers, but bad for tourism. Changing the crops grown would change the bird life, and this could damage bird watching.

One person who has become active in the debate over Beit Netofa Valley is Laithi Ganaim. He studied environmental programmes at the university affiliated Arava Institute, and returned to Sakhnin determined to create environmental improvement at grass roots level. His Food Bank Farm Project in Beit Netofa asks families to give one hour of work per week and in return they receive vegetables. During the first year they must learn to grow their own food and then go on to support another family. They have 22 dunam of wheat and chickpeas, for which they pay only 100 shekels per dunam per year, a comparatively low price. Through his contacts with various foundations, Laithi provides the land, seed and instruction.

The aim is to create an organic co-operative, but certification would cost more than they can afford at present. One way to get around this is to begin marketing within their very large extended families. Even more ambitiously, Laithi wants a system for rainwater catchment in Beit Netofa, but he has been waiting for over a year for permission.

Laithi is not prepared to work together with TAEQ in trying to solve these issues. He regards TAEQ as an enforcement agency, set up by the government, and he maintained that he is opposed to many of their goals. However, I found it difficult to see where the disagreement lay. This was a great pity, as he is a highly intelligent, skilled and educated grass roots activist, who has already created valuable projects which are benefiting local people.

On one of the hills overlooking Beit Netofa, Yuval Steinberg runs an organic goat farm and cheese-making dairy. He combines this with education and programmes for schools and kindergartens. He told me that his aim is to get children and nature together. He demonstrated an interesting grazing method, where he moves his flock relatively quickly across the scrub, allowing them to eat the low shrubs, but leaving the small trees alone. This encourages the trees to grow, hopefully resulting in a more developed ecosystem. He makes soft, low-salt cheese, with herbs and spices, using milk from his own goats and in addition milk bought in from local dairies. There is an increasing demand for natural goat's cheese, especially low-salt. He also offers courses in different places, often bringing some animals with him.

Yuval's farm is a good example of diversified organic farming, combining education and care of the land with producing a good wholesome product increasingly in demand.

Not far from Yuval's farm Jonatan Ritter has a small workshop where he produces perfumes distilled from wild, locally growing herbs. He began experimenting with this at Kibbutz Lotan deep in the Arava desert twenty-five years ago. He moved up here to Galilee about fifteen years ago, doing a variety of jobs, including teaching Permaculture. Jonatan and I ran workshops for TAEQ on Permaculture way back in the early days. Today he has concentrated his efforts on distilling herbs and blending his own perfumes, most of which he sells directly, trying as much as possible to cut out the middlemen. This is giving him and his family a reasonable living in one of the most beautiful places in Israel.

Both Yuval and Jonatan are good examples of how we can achieve rural development, combining skills with business and at the same time taking care of the environment. This is the kind of development TAEQ is actively trying to encourage through its planning activities.

Organic farming in the Sakhnin valley

Jonatan Ritter demonstrating his perfume distillery to a visiting group of Palestinians

Gasan Ganaim (not to be confused with Bassem Ganaim, portrayed in this chapter) is the only employee of the Amutat ha Bustan, an organization of twenty-three farmers with about 200 dunam of land who obtain their water from the treated wastewater at TAEQ. Gasan works part-time managing the water system. The rest of his income comes from growing fruit on about 15 dunam. In addition he has about the same amount of land in olive trees, mainly for oil. The olives are grown organically, cultivating the ground to keep the weeds down in the traditional Arab manner. The fruit is grown using chemicals and sold to a local contractor from Nazareth. He has many different varieties in order to spread the work of managing the trees, and the harvesting of the produce.

Amutat Ha Bustan could expand, taking in more land and more farmers, but this would need extra investment, which they don't have at present. The project is the result of an initiative started by TAEQ in order to use the treated wastewater. There were problems of acceptability to be overcome to begin with, but these seem to have been solved, and there are plans to put in the infrastructure for an extra 1,000 dunam.

In the inevitable switch from chemical to organic agriculture, TAEQ is certainly aligning itself with the winners, but it has not yet realized its full potential as a leading player in the actual switch.

Above left: Gasan Ganaim with one of the filters for the processed sewage water
Above right: Olive groves
Below left: Wild flowers growing between the olives in spring
Below right: Gasan Ganaim showing one of his grafted fruit saplings

Portrait of Bassem Ganaim

Bassem Ganaim

Bassem is a young, good looking guy, and it is hard to believe that he has already been married for fourteen years, has three children and one more on the way. He went to school in Sakhnin and was good at maths, physics and biology, but he left before completing his education. He used to work in building, but after he had an accident, Hussein arranged for him to work at TAEQ.

Bassem comes from the biggest clan in Sakhnin, who have been here for many generations. When he was a kid, there were far fewer houses here, and many more open spaces for playing in. His father said that life here was better before, even without electricity or phones. There were fewer problems then and he wishes it could return to that again.

He has worked here for ten years and is in charge of all kinds of maintenance jobs. He is very involved with the LIFE Project, and that is what he's most proud of. He fixes whatever needs fixing, but also helps the students with their projects, samples, tests and results. Whatever needs doing, he'll always fix it 'in five minutes', even if it takes several days!

It is not always easy to reason with Bassem. He has a proud demeanour, and feels the responsibility of his position. 'Bassem knows best' is a trait that marks his work at the Centre. He always looks optimistic, and when asked about the future replied with a big smile, 'Things are good here and will get even better!'

9. 'The Green Building' with the Blue Towers

The site at Sakhnin is a dynamic, ever changing place. While we were working on this book during the first half of 2008, the office wing of the new building was gradually nearing completion. By the time this book is published, the present office building will be the old office building, but it still has a story to tell, part of the development of skills and ideas that make up the biography of TAEQ.

The (old) office building was like a trial run in ecological architecture. Originally TAEQ was located in town, until it was decided to make the point that there was no problem locating next to the waste-

The Green Building with its blue towers

water treatment plant on the outskirts of Sakhnin. At first the office was housed in a temporary caravan, and then in 1998 the staff at TAEQ rescued concrete panels, doors and windows from a school building that was being demolished in Sakhnin. They used the minimum of money. The roof was made of corrugated metal, with two centimetres of polystyrene insulation, and plastic on top of that as noise insulation against the winter rain. The walls were thickened with mud and straw bales on the outside for insulation. They planted vines on the south side as shade against the summer sun and plastered adobe on the inside of the walls for thermal mass. This building was done in several workshops, with trials, research and experiments. They tried, unsuccessfully, putting in underground air conditioning. This failure later led them to experiment with the Malkaf system, of which we shall hear more later.

The construction of the office initiated research and education on ecological building, with the participation of both students and community volunteers. In 2002 a start was made on a new ecological building which was going to house offices, classrooms, laboratories, lecture halls and public areas. Several energy-conserving elements, based on traditional and modern planning, were incorporated into the design and architecture of this building. The effectiveness of these elements was investigated by local students, under the supervision of the staff at TAEQ. These elements were found to impact significantly on the energy consumption of the building.

The building's roots go back much further, however. In the early 1990s Abed Yassen and Riyad Dwere were colleagues in an architectural office in Araba. They incorporated a lot of traditional ideas in their work, but it was Riyad who was interested in combining this with ecological aspects. The planning and first drawings of the new building started in 1995. Abed and Riyad told us how the building attained its present form. Originally a grant was forthcoming from the Ministry of Education for a seminar centre, based on the work that TAEQ was doing with high school students. The grant came with conditions, which determined the layout and design of the building, and which government approved contractors could carry out the work. Abed suggested dispensing with the plans, the list of contractors and the grant. 'Let's take a white sheet of paper and create our dreams out of our fantasies!' The Green Building materialized, and money was found from alternative sources, while building costs were kept down by utilizing the labour of the staff at TAEQ, of students, work groups and of people doing community service. After many years of

During construction in 2006, the concrete frame of the Green Building is clearly visible

planning and preparation, work started in 2002.

Riyad and Abed initiated several different groups to start researching into this kind of building. They looked into traditional buildings in local towns and villages to check out cooling systems, angles of the sun, temperatures, wind and moisture. They studied from other resources such as books and the Internet, incorporating their results into the design of the building.

Before each part of the building was done, they held workshops trying out materials they intended to use. For example, Riyad incorporated techniques he remembered from his childhood that he had learnt from his grandmother, when he used to help her make the traditional *tabun* (bread oven) out of mud and straw. The whole building process was an educational experience.

The Green Building was constructed using natural materials such as local stones, soil, straw, and stabilized lime, similar to the traditional construction in the area. These materials were combined with concrete for the main frame, to carry the weight of the various components. In addition, planning and construction are adapted to the topography and are based on local wind flow and sun angle.

One of the essential features of the Green Building is the inner courtyard, the Riwaq or cloister. It serves as a cooling or warming area, depending on the season, and it works day and night in all seasons. In summer, cool air comes in at night and circulates. There are windows all round the inner courtyard. These open at ground level to let in the maximum of cool air at night, and are double glazed for thermal efficiency. In winter they protect from the cold winds and let in the heat of the sun. There is a large water cistern in the middle of the courtyard, also a very traditional feature, used for watering plants and filling pots. There are four large date palms in the courtyard which provide added symmetry and cast shadows around the main area, cooling it during the day. By mid-afternoon, the doors of the rooms facing the main area are opened, to create a transfer of the relatively cooler air from the rooms to the main area and upward, creating a slight, but noticeable breeze. A great deal of research was done on traditional courtyards throughout the local area in order to obtain concrete scientific evidence of the behaviour of this feature.

Probably the most striking visual aspect of the Green Building is the three blue towers that can be seen from far away. These are the cooling towers, *malqaf* in Arabic, a traditional and simple technology which has been in use throughout the Middle East for centuries, if not millennia. It operates on the principle of transferring air from the upper opening to the lower opening, where the rooms are located. Spraying water into the internal space of the *malqaf* causes the air to

Homemade mud bricks ready to be used in internal wall construction to create thermal mass

Right: The courtyard of the Green Building with the water fountain in the middle

Riyad showing the small windows before the frames were installed

cool faster and increases its falling velocity. A great deal of research was done here, to do with the optimal height in connection with the building, taking all variables into consideration. With the aid of these towers the temperature can be reduced from 36 to 22°C. If the air is dry, the cooling process is more efficient. This is a low impact way of cooling buildings, using simple technology. It is becoming popular throughout the Permaculture network, as it becomes better known.

The roof of the Green Building also sports domes and half cylinder vaults. They take longer to heat up because of their larger surface areas. They have good acoustics and are strong constructions. They receive light via attractive coloured glass known as *tizanas* (natural light bulbs). These were made especially for the project, with blue glass from Hebron. The bulbous shape of the glass facing outside the dome brings in more light than a simple flat-paned window. The concentrated natural light illuminates the central areas of the building, and research has shown they reduce the need for artificial light to just a few hours a day. Throughout the day, the sides of the domes and vaults are heated by the sun, creating an upward stream of air. This stream allows the cooler air to remain at the bottom of the dome, and in the communal areas underneath. Windows then allow hot air to escape outside the building.

The many small windows located throughout the building help to further increase the movement and speed of air flow. While the total area of the windows is equal to the area of one large window, the multiple windows create more shadows. They let air in, but with the minimum of heat.

Throughout the building carpenters were busy during the early summer installing *mashrabia* or wooden screens. These have several functions. They can be opened to admire the view. They cool the heat of the sun and they take out dampness (the word *mashrabia* comes from the Arabic word 'to drink').

The building was by no means finished during the time we lived at Sakhnin. A large complex of classrooms and courtyards was due to be added to the eastern side, while the whole of the south-facing wall will be a greenhouse, which will let hot air into the building in winter. As we watched, $60m^2$ of photovoltaic cells were being added on the roof, some standing straight, others at an angle. The idea is to install different systems, some for electricity and some for hot water, all for research. The aim is to attain zero energy consumption. As it is these environmental strategies result in a saving of 72% in energy costs

Mashrabia shutters on the Green Building

Installing the photovoltaic cells on the roof of the Green Building

according to recent research. The total annual energy consumption today is around 68,000 kWh/y, while the total energy consumption of a standard building of the same size is 246,000 kWh/y. When the Green Building is finished it is estimated that its total annual energy consumption will be about 19 000 kWh/y. (All figures from the *Israel Environmental Bulletin,* Volume 32, May 2007, published by the Israel Ministry of Environmental Protection.)

The Green Building proudly demonstrating its international repute

The Green Building surrounded by landscaped gardens

Financially the project has been very successful. Conventionally, the total cost of the building would have been about $2 million, but with savings made by using used materials, garbage, and own labour, the real cost was about half of that. In addition every year over two hundred pupils do research on the building.

Everyone at TAEQ is justifiably proud of the Green Building. In 2005 there was an Environmental Convention in Japan where sixty countries participated, and the Green Building represented Israel. A year later the Green Building won first prize in the MED-ENEC Competition out of thirty-one entries from countries around the Mediterranean. Winning the MED-ENEC prize led to contacts with many other countries and people.

By having to build an office, and later a custom-designed seminar centre, TAEQ became involved in serious environmental building research and development. This has added a substantial field of activity to their educational arsenal, and has gained them international recognition. The people working on this have become some of the leaders of this field in Israel, and are being taken seriously by both mainstream planners and alternative Permaculture designers. We all have a great deal to learn here.

Portrait of Abed Yassen

Abed Yassen

Abed is of small stature, dapper, with dark sparkling eyes. A strong, compact and sturdy character, reflected in his characterful building.

He is one of ten children of a Muslim schoolteacher from Araba, every one of whom went on to study at university level. His father studied at the University of Beirut, and when he finally returned to Araba he surprised everyone by marrying a woman who had no formal education. Abed spoke proudly of the strong and mutually respectful relationship between his parents.

Abed himself went on to study architecture in Italy, and was inspired by Hassan Fathi, an Egyptian architect who came to Turin as visiting Professor in the early and mid-1980s. Upon his return to Israel, Abed worked at a doctorate in Building Preservation at the Technion in Haifa, carrying on with Fathi's work, documenting it and trying to give a 'scientific framework' to old buildings, to formalize them under the title 'What is Modern?' He managed to visit Egypt and Hassan Fathi before the latter's death in 1989. Abed comments, 'Hassan Fathi was unknown here until relatively recently, and is very controversial.'

Abed is concerned with combining ecological awareness with cultural traditions. He is not a Sufi, but likes the Sufi way of thinking and uses it in his design. He feels that the Arabs in this region have suffered a great deal, and for him the Green Building is a 'cry', a shout of pain. 'Without suffering you cannot create', Abed commented. He needs to shout that we can build in other ways, that we can do lots of things in other ways. This society is full of segregation, ghettos and divisions. He doesn't want even more borders. This building has identity. 'I can also dance my own dance. There is soul to this building. If you don't feel it, you will pass in and out and through it just like the wind.'

Portrait of Riyad Dwere

Riyad is a smiling, quiet and calm man who always seems to have the time of day for you. He is a family man from Eilabun, proud of his Muslim background, but no longer practising.

He studied Building Engineering at Tel Khai College and then at the Technion in Haifa, going on to work in an architectural office in Sakhnin on environmental planning and other projects.

In the early 1990s he realized that a centre such as this was needed, but saw the difficulties ahead. This was before the instant access to

Riyad Dwere

communication and information which came with the spread of the Internet a few years later. Personally he wanted very much to be involved in developing the ideas for TAEQ, so he started to work part-time on this project. Since 1998 he has worked here full-time, but continues with private projects, always with an ecological connection. At the Centre he is responsible for site development and planning.

The project that is closest to his heart is without a doubt the Green Building. This for Riyad is not only about the physical building itself, but the effect it has had already on the surroundings and in Israel itself. When they received first prize for the project in the MED-ENEC competition in 2006, it came both as a surprise and a stroke of good luck. People already knew of TAEQ before this event, but afterwards more people got to hear about it, including architects and engineers. While doing research for this book, I travelled with Riyad to a national meeting of Israeli builders and architects on the subject of environmental building using earth, clay and lime, and his presentation, the only one from an Arab, was warmly and enthusiastically received.

Riyad does not need a lot of persuading to show you the engineering details of the Green Building, and before you know it, he is widening his scope, showing you private houses that he has designed using some of the techniques researched at the centre. Talking of building with earth and straw, he acknowledges his debt to his family; 'I learnt how to build with mud from my grandmother, helping her make bread ovens in our family courtyard when I was a kid!'

Riyad demonstrating the lower windows opening on to the courtyard

10. The International Web

Winning the MED-ENEC prize for the Green Building in 2006 certainly helped TAEQ become known internationally. However, contact with other countries had already been well established before then. Many people, academics and professionals working on environmental issues know about the Sakhnin project, both in Israel and the world at large. The foreign connections were and still are mainly at university level, but a good deal of academic research has been carried out in conjunction with local Israeli universities. Work has been done at master's and doctorate level by students from the Technion (Haifa), Haifa University, Tel Aviv University, University of the Negev (Ben Gurion), by Ort Braude College at Karmiel, and Tel Khai College in the Upper Galilee. TAEQ itself has no funding for this, the research projects having to come with their own budgets.

Contact with Turkey started in 2002, when Hussein attended an international conference on wastewater treatment held in Istanbul. He met Professor Izzet Izturk and they collaborated on creating a research project in Sakhnin. In 2003 and in 2006 there were post-doctorate students working in Sakhnin for one year each. There are some areas of Turkey that are well endowed with water, but other areas with very little, so the idea of recycling wastewater is highly relevant to them and environmental engineering has become an important subject. The LIFE Project, described in Chapter 7, was conceived as a joint project with Turkey, financed by a grant from the European Union. In 2005 there was a seminar about the development of rural technological research, which led to Turkish post-doctorate students coming to

Shlomo at one of the experimental sites for treating sewage

TAEQ. The University of Istanbul is also involved, sending a master's student here each year. This has been a great success, with one student publishing five academic papers during the ten months he was doing research here. There is still an excellent connection with Turkey and the intention is to continue with it.

Connections with Germany are more to do with alternative energy and rural planning. The Israeli office of Industry, Commerce and Labour initiated one of these projects, basing their interest in putting alternative energy into action. Shlomo and Hussein followed this up by contacting the Labour Office in Germany. They hope that courses on this subject will begin soon. An Israeli student connected to the LINK Foundation, described in Chapter 4, studied Regional Planning at Göttingen University, which led to PhD students from there coming to Sakhnin to look at environmental economics, eco-tourism and conservation and then submitting joint applications for European Union programmes. Additional connections were made with the

German Ministries of Trade and of Education through the winning of the MED-ENEC prize.

This prize also created links with Donau University at Krems in Austria. An energy engineer came to visit, and Shlomo and Hussein returned the visit in 2007. There are now discussions about organizing a three-way joint programme between TAEQ, Ben Gurion University and the Donau University at Krems on the subjects of energy conservation and traditional building. .

In the mid-1990s the Ford Foundation gave TAEQ a grant for technological equipment. Being a modest sum, it was used to install water infrastructure and equipment for the laboratory, bringing it up to required educational standards, and it gave the Centre just what was needed to begin the serious educational and research work that has later developed and blossomed.

For the last three years students have been coming from George Mason University in Virginia to do their internships. About thirty students have been here for a month in the summer, and in the winter. This connection with George Mason University will be further consolidated when Hussein takes up his post-doctoral research at the university in the autumn of 2008, for at least one year.

Closer to home there have been some connections with Jordan, with groups of professional engineers coming to Sakhnin for seminars. One of the results of these meetings has been the Partnership for Peace programme, described in Chapter 4. There is a strong desire to continue with these contacts, especially with the Jordanian University for Science and Technology, who are interested in biogas and in reviewing the building laws, creating new guidelines for environmental building.

There is also a plan being developed now to initiate a joint Young Leadership Programme in the field of energy conservation and renewable energy application, together with students from both Jordan and Germany. The idea is to implement the project as a 'pilot educational model' in all three countries in parallel. This would require close co-operation of a multi-disciplinary team of experts and teachers in fields such as architecture, engineering, handicrafts, physics and biotechnology. This team would create educational programmes for high school students in all the participating countries. In addition, a series of one week workshops are planned to be held during the summer vacations as part of this programme.

On a less academic, more at a grassroots level, is the connection with the Solar Village of Tamera in Portugal. This is based on a community founded in 1995 as an intentional research centre in the subject of community and social living. Tamera now has about two hundred co-workers committed to building up social and technical models that can be replicated in other parts of the world. One of their initiatives involves building a Peace Research Village in the Middle East, hopefully on the border between Israel and the Palestinian Authority. They have gradually built up a strong network and are supporting a core group of Israelis and Palestinians currently at Tamera, who will eventually carry this project into fruition.

In March 2008, Sabine Lichtenfels and Charly Rainer Ehrenpreis, founders of Tamera, came to visit TAEQ while on a tour of Israel and the Palestinian areas. They were impressed by the Green Building and spent time talking with Riyad about ecological building technology in general. Whether this will blossom into another area of co-operation and exchange remains to be seen, but it is these visits, sometimes regarded as chance meetings, that create the web of international contacts that we see developing at TAEQ.

My own presence at Sakhnin, living there for half a year, teaching and writing, has created its own set of potential joint projects. This book itself is another stimulant, and it is certainly one of my hopes that people reading this will be interested to make contact with TAEQ and initiate new areas of co-operation.

Portrait of Shlomo Kimchie

Shlomo commutes irregularly from Haifa a few days a week, a trip of about forty-five minutes if the traffic is not too bad. Short, compact and sprightly, with a passion for Israeli folk dancing, he has officially retired, but carries on as a freelance adviser.

Originally from a Jewish family in Jerusalem, where he completed his master's degree in Biotechnology, he subsequently came to Haifa Technion, hoping he would be able to turn his studies into something more useful. He finished his doctorate in 1985 on how to treat cow manure through anaerobic processes. He then turned to research into treating coal fly ash, a waste product from the Israeli coal-fired power stations. In the bad old days this was merely dumped into the Mediterranean, but when it was discovered that the ash was highly toxic, Greenpeace put pressure on the National Electricity Company to find other solutions.

It was through this project that Shlomo met Hussein, a young student whom he invited to do his master's degree research on how to leach out the various toxic minerals from the fly ash and turn them into recyclable materials. When Hussein was considering taking up the directorship of TAEQ, Shlomo encouraged him, suggesting that further studies at doctorate level could always be done later.

Today Shlomo is the scientific manager at TAEQ and responsible for international relations. From the beginning, it had been the intention of TAEQ to be a joint Arab-Jewish venture, with a strong input of dialogue and co-operation, and Shlomo is concerned to carry on working consciously in this direction.

Shlomo showing one of the sand filters

Illegal garbage dumping just outside Sakhnin

11. Not Just Teaching

Nearly every day, people came to visit the Centre. During the half year that we stayed in Sakhnin, we were the only people actually living on site, in the old laboratory building, past its prime, but spacious and comfortable enough for us. We saw the buses pulling in most days, the car park full of cars, and the quiet that descended upon the place in the late afternoon when everyone left. There were young schoolchildren, high school and university students, nurses, lawyers and a continuously varied stream of visitors from far-flung places.

As Mukhles put it, 'There are many projects, and they are not all educational. The Centre tries to involve itself with the outside world and does not just sit and wait for people to come here.'

They have gone beyond just advising teachers how to present environmental issues in schools. For example, nurses from a Well Baby Clinic are learning about the environment, and about the medicines and poisons they may be using in their clinics. There is an educational programme for housewives and mothers, so that they too will be better informed about these issues and can in turn start educating their own children. There is outreach to lawyers, who need constant updating on new environmental laws and how to deal with public hazards and complaints.

TAEQ is a busy and demanding workplace. There are about a dozen people full-time on the staff, and each person has a role, which often carries with it several areas of responsibility. For example, Riyad's main work is in environmental planning, but he also leads research and teaches. Everyone has more than a full-time schedule, and gives their maximum. It is the people that make for the success of the place, and they all support each other.

Regional Environmental Units like TAEQ were set up originally to be the long arm of the Ministry of the Environment, making sure that government directives were carried out, inspecting the distant corners of the land. It was Hussein's idea to add educational and research elements to this original task. At TAEQ, it is Saleh Waked who is responsible for being public inspector. He informs people on methods of dealing with plant infestation. He inspects businesses in the private and public sectors on environmental issues, and he deals with complaints from the public, giving fines when necessary. However, he tries hard to tackle the actual problem first, and only if that does not succeed, does he resort to prosecution. He has worked in this field for seven years, and maintains he has made no real enemies. He always goes to the specific place and talks politely to people face to face, explaining the issues at hand and how to deal with them correctly in order to reach a satisfactory compromise. Only if there is no co-operation does he resort to legal action. Of course, like everyone else who works there he also gives lectures and is involved in the educational programmes.

We asked him about some of his successful environmental actions, and he told us a string of stories. About the time he closed a concrete factory in Araba, and the marble factory in Sakhnin that met the same fate. He is proud of his success in moving a car repair workshop from a residential area in Sakhnin to an industrial area nearby. Once he prosecuted a local mayor who neglected his duties when there was a strike and the main water system was turned off. Some of this mayor's council workers had received no wages for one and a half years. Saleh succeeded in getting the Green Police to open a personal file on this mayor. Once, in one day, he handed out fines to various people to the tune of 15,000 shekels! (About $4,500 at the time of writing.)

A few years ago there was a trip out for all the pupils from one of the Sakhnin schools and afterwards it appeared that about fifty of them had reported sick and been hospitalized. They had been poisoned by a particular breed of caterpillar that nests in certain pine trees. Saleh immediately contacted the local council and informed other official bodies. The area was closed off by the authorities, and the infestation dealt with in the correct way. He was interviewed on local television about this incident.

There are a number of smaller projects, each one of which would be a major feature in its own right, but at TAEQ they are dwarfed by the size of the whole operation.

The Municipalities Programme is designed to create Centres of Local Sustainability, where each municipality must elect its own environmental committee which comes to the Centre for lectures and tours. Currently TAEQ works with nine municipalities of which three are from the local region. This project is Hanadi's particular responsibility.

The Kimama Project is run in connection with the Arava Institute, which is located at Kibbutz Ktura in the Arava desert near Eilat. This project involves about thirty-six Arabs and Jews who come together from all over the country, every weekend, to train as leaders for an eco-camp to be held in the summer, near Tiberias on the shores of the Sea of Galilee.

The Coalition for the Advancement of Environmental Education for Arabs and Jews does pretty much what its title implies. In this project the emphasis is on planning together. The tendency is for initiatives to come from the Jewish sector and to be translated and passed on to the Arabs. Visions, goals, workshops and websites need to be built together.

The Galillead Project also works on creating a dialogue between Arabs and Jews. Their focus is not so much technological as sociological. One of their participants was Roza Ghanim from Sajur, one of the Druze mountain villages on the slopes of Mount Meron. She worked together with Racheli Ivkar from the Jewish village of Shorashim. They had seen a need to create a supportive environment for mentally and physically handicapped people in this region, and were designing a project which would combine a small farm with handicraft workshops and a visitors' centre. Here Jewish, Druze and Arab people with special needs could work together, produce useful and beautiful products, and contribute to society.

As a volunteer at TAEQ, I was asked to contribute to their outreach programme. During the first week I was there, I got a call from the office telling me that the police were here looking for me. Fearing the worst, I turned up at the main office, to find myself being invited on a site visit and preliminary consultation at the Khermon Prison. This meeting led to a half-day seminar on Permaculture planning with practical planning exercises for prison directors from the north of Israel. There were eight prisons represented, and five draft plans were presented at the end of the seminar. It was recommended that this be followed up by further seminars or consultations.

A similar situation arose with the Misgav Regional Council, where I was invited to a consultancy meeting with a number of teachers at the local school, resulting in a half-day seminar for kindergarten teachers, building a Permaculture mulch garden. I was invited to another site visit on a kibbutz where a meditation group was planning an ecological meditation centre. They subsequently came to the TAEQ site to see environmental building strategies and wastewater treatment systems.

Just like the international contacts, these local relationships are often the result of chance meetings, personal contacts and the seemingly serendipitous encounters which happen to us all. In the larger picture, this creates a web of people working together and supporting each other.

Portrait of Saleh Waked

Saleh Waked

Saleh is true to his Arabic name, meaning upright or honest. He is one of the unsung heroes of the Centre. Not open to bribery or corruption, he works only for the good of the community. Ever eager to improve his English, he also speaks a fine Hebrew. He is a cool customer indeed, tall, suave and good looking, his freshly ironed light blue shirt complementing his unusual pale blue-green eyes. He has a quiet and diplomatic air about him, essential for his sensitive job. He is the inspector for environmental transgressions and will fine both friend and foe alike. One of his most renowned triumphs was fining a policeman for littering the sidewalk with his spent cigarette butt, only split seconds after being fined himself for illegal use of his mobile phone whilst driving.

Saleh is the only member of staff from the nearby village of Araba, where his Muslim family has lived for generations. He studied in Tel Aviv, specializing in Pest Control, Agricultural Environmental Engineering, and Treatment of Dangerous Materials, such as asbestos and fluoride gases. At TAEQ his primary role is as public inspector and he commands a standby team to deal with environmental emergencies. He also gives lectures, and is involved in the educational programmes.

12. An Environmental Flagship

Karmiel is a modern Israeli, Jewish town only a few miles from Sakhnin. Over the past decades the Arabs of Sakhnin, Araba and Deir Hana have watched land being made available and money being poured into creating this new town. At the same time, they feel their own land is being squeezed, and that there is a lack of finances for their own development. The common land around the valley of Sakhnin has been taken for building new Jewish settlements, villages that have plenty of space for new neighbourhoods, new kindergartens and schools. Arabs whose forefathers grazed their flocks on this very land cannot settle in these villages, despite ongoing court cases and legal decisions.

There is a serious lack of equality between Arabs and Jews in Israel.

The projects being worked on in Sakhnin need to be seen against this background, but it is a good deal more complicated than the comments above seem to indicate. In absolute terms the Arabs in Israel are much better off than Arabs in most countries of the Middle East. They have a higher standard of living, better health care and better education. They can vote in local and national elections and travel to most countries in the world on their Israeli passports. But this may not be a cause for comfort. In the absolute worst case scenario of Israel being conquered by its Arab neighbours, the Jewish population being either slaughtered or deported, what might happen to those Arabs who 'collaborated' with the Zionist entity? Those who worked for government departments like TAEQ? Those who worked for Jewish companies and made a good living? Those who studied at Jewish universities and became highly successful professionals? This is a serious concern, and a source of tension between Palestinians living within the Palestinian Authority and their Israeli Arab cousins. The Arabs who have stayed in Israel and received Israeli citizenship are not allowed entrance into many Arab countries.

Despite these gloomy observations, optimism is rife. One person we talked to commented, 'Peace will come. There is no choice. It is the only direction. How much time are we wasting? The Jews and the Arabs are so close genetically.' Another said, 'There are good people here. We have good schools and colleges in comparison with other towns around here. This is a strong area in a democratic land.'

There is no doubt about the overcrowding, however. There are few openings for widespread development and there are financial constraints. The industrial area in Sakhnin is too small and overcrowded and this is a cause of many environmental problems. For example, the waste garbage from demolished buildings could be broken down for recycling, but there is no such facility. The town feels financially undeveloped and even though the problems are visible, the people feel helpless to do anything about them. In Araba, there is still no industrial area. There is simply not enough land. Maybe there are political reasons for this. The local Misgav council does not give support or financial aid, even though there are ten times as many inhabitants in the Sakhnin/Araba area as in Misgav. There is an unfair distribution of land and finances. Hussein is also aware of this and thinks that in the meantime the land between Sakhnin and Araba can be developed, but this should be for organic farming, eco-tourism and general green development rather than for housing and industry.

While we were living in Sakhnin, there were several people who spent time working at TAEQ for their community service, sometimes in addition to paying off fines or spending time in prison. Some of them had been prosecuted for illegal building, and one of them explained that the people in Sakhnin don't have enough space to build. They say they are not allowed to build on their own land that was given to them by their grandfathers. One young man had to pay a fine of 50,000 shekels (about $15,000 at the time of writing) plus four months' social service for building illegally. It had taken him two years to pay off the fine. He told us that here in Sakhnin they don't bulldoze illegal building, either you must pull it down yourself, or pay for the labour and machinery if the authorities do it.

There are many groups and projects working to solve these problems at TAEQ. The people on the staff are aware that peace and environment go together. The team is serious about what they are working for here and care very much about improving the quality of life for the local communities. Future generations should benefit from their work.

Riyad calls for more research for ecological building, Jewish-Arab co-operation and eco-tourism. He thinks that this should be a place where like-minded people can gather from all over the Mediterranean and the rest of the world to carry on working on these issues. Jummana is convinced that the Centre will continue to grow, and become even more important in the region than it already is. Mukhles is proud that he has been able to maintain the high number of schools and student visitors here, in spite of growing competition from other establishments. He is continually renewing his ideas and educational programmes. There are new initiatives starting up here all the time, and he manages to incorporate these into the educational side of things. He is frustrated that he has not yet managed to have as much contact as he wants to with similar projects or people from abroad. Most of the high school students that come here are from the Arab, not the Jewish, sector and he would like it to be more balanced. There was a connection with a Jewish school in Tiv'on, but they have stopped coming as they feel they can tackle similar work themselves. At the beginning of the project, it was difficult to attract younger children from elementary schools, but now they do come, enjoy themselves and want to return. Mukhles aims to cover as many subjects as possible, so that the centre will become more and more self-sufficient, with less need to search elsewhere. He aims to cover topics such as organic agriculture, research on air, and sound pollution. Every year he has something new to offer, and wants the Centre to be known for being effective and well organized. Hanadi still dreams of developing an animal park that will allow children to connect with the animals through personal contact. This would allow children with special needs to be exposed to environmental issues through first-hand experiences.

Many of those that work at TAEQ are well aware of the key role that Hussein has played, and continues to play, in moving things along. When asked about the future, Said commented, 'Without Hussein, this place would not happen. He is strong and always thinks of the future.' Bassem added, 'This place is unique. Hussein manages to get donations from all over the world to keep it going. We respect Hussein. If it wasn't for Hussein, this place would have closed long ago. He puts his heart into it. Things are good here and will get even better!' Haim Shinhar, one of the original founders described in Chapter 2, was even more specific when asked about the future, 'Hussein should one day become the mayor of Sakhnin and his influence will spread far and wide!'

According to ex-mayor Mustafa Abu Raya, the biggest and most important contribution of TAEQ is guidance and education. He believes people here must regain their 'philosophy of life' and get back in contact with nature. One way of doing this is by recreational walking, and the Centre could develop more paths and bike tracks. People should also have the opportunity for developing more agriculture. The environment should enter into the soul of every inhabitant. He wants Sakhnin to lead in these areas, first in the Galilee, then in Israel, then in the world. It is true that the town has received a lot of support from the Ministry of the Environment, not because Sakhnin is liked, but because the money is used well, and the results are visible. It is used as a good example. TAEQ has already received support from the European Union. Mustafa sees it as being a serious and professional place.

From his many years as mayor, Mustafa is bitter when it comes to the place of Arabs in Israel. He feels that the Arabs are not really wanted here, and are not allowed to develop. He pointed out that Sakhnin is centrally placed and yet has no hospital or university. Instead, Nahariya and Kiryat Ata (Jewish towns along the coast) are being developed. People from Sakhnin have to travel elsewhere for these services, and it should be the other way round. In this region twice as many Arabs as Jews work in the medical profession, and that should be reflected in the building of a hospital here.

Jamal Tarabeah's comment was short and to the point. He said, 'We all live here and we must co-operate. We can be friends. I want peace.' He went on to point out that of course there are many good Jews in Israel, but when people believe that this land was given to them by God this becomes a problem. He wants to move forward from the Old Testament and from the Koran. Unless there is real forgiveness, the arguments will continue.

Haim Shinhar voiced an opinion which originally had inspired me to write about this centre. He sees the environmental project as a way to get Jews and Arabs to work together. He considers co-operation between different cultures to be one of the key contributions that TAEQ has to make. Can the threat of environmental degradation be stronger than the internal conflicts which dominate the Middle East? Can co-operation in environmental work be a tool for communication within a multicultural society? Is this something which can pull people together to solve common problems? Haim wants these questions to form the starting point for real change here in the Middle East.

Like Mustafa, Jamal and Haim, Shlomo has a long-term perspective on the work that is being carried out at the Centre. He has seen a steady improvement and growth since 1993, a growth that must keep on advancing. The Centre has its impact on the Council, the town, the schoolchildren, and on all the hundreds of people who have passed through here. There are students now interested in doing postgraduate research on the social influence and on the psychological impact of the projects being carried out by TAEQ. They could go far, both Arabs and Jews alike. And everything escalated from the idea of sewage pools! The Centre has turned into a flagship for the environment in the whole of Israel, in spite of all the difficulties. A certain critical mass of highly qualified engineers and scientists is needed here, professional people who can see a good future with high quality equipment, laboratories and support. The Centre is now working in conjunction with Ort Braude College in Karmiel. This helps to make TAEQ more professional and attractive, where people can do hands-on research into water and the environment. It takes years to build up these connections.

Yussuf Ganaim, the night guard, put it most simply when asked about the future. 'God willing, there will be peace. Peace is better, we should all live together.'

Portrait of Yussuf Ganaim

If you arrive at the Centre after dark, the person that you are most likely to meet is Yussuf Ganaim, his red and white traditional keffiya wrapped in a swirl around his head. He is the night guard, alternating between patrolling the extensive grounds with his dog Rex, and in his guardhouse by the gate, making some of the best coffee you will ever taste.

He is the oldest employee, with a varied working background, in restaurants, in building, and as doorman at the local council offices. His connections to the Centre go back to Jamal Tarabeah, mayor of Sakhnin when the Centre was first discussed, and he knew Hussein from these early days. He has been working here as night guard for the last seven years.

A devout Muslim, he plans to go on the Haj to Mecca with his wife in the autumn of 2008. His son played in the Bnei Sakhnin football team, and he has always lived in the town.

Yussuf is a born storyteller, and he brings his stories alive. He tells about people who try to make a nuisance of themselves at night, of Sakhnin characters, and of events in his life. He weaves sagas and epics out of the simplest tales, filling the room with larger than life characters, conversations and action. He is a one man show, a veritable theatrical performer.

Yussuf Ganaim

Afterthoughts

During the six months we were in Sakhnin, collecting material and writing this book, events in the country were not really uplifting. From Gaza, rockets were shot at Sderot and Ashkelon, killing Israeli civilians, while the Israeli army was busy killing Palestinians in return. Eight Yeshiva (Jewish religious school) students were shot by Palestinian extremists in Jerusalem one evening, and life became increasingly harder for the Palestinians in the occupied territories. Listening to the news on the radio gave little hope for a peaceful solution.

Among the hundreds of people that we came into contact with there was an overwhelming majority who just wanted peace. A peace which would give them security and dignity to carry on normal lives, earning enough to give their families a decent life. We also met others who gave us less hope. Jews who didn't trust the Arabs, and Arabs who blamed the Zionists for their present predicament. Muslims who disliked the Druze, and Christians who complained about the Bedouin. And then there were those who were quite prepared to live in a constant state of war for however long it took to have their claims satisfied, with no willingness to compromise.

As I came to realize that peace must be built from the three pillars of politics, economics and culture, I saw the value of the small steps that were being taken at Sakhnin. Clearly there are no easy solutions. Peace must be sought, not only on the political level, but also between individuals getting to know each other and breaking down their damaging stereotypes, and on the economic level, creating co-operation by trading and doing business together. The environmental Centre in Sakhnin is not a political initiative. It is engaged in bringing people together, people who are already open to meeting across the political, religious and ethnic fault lines of the Middle East. By bringing them together we have a hope that this in itself will break down destructive images, and may even stimulate them to develop productive relationships.

Even if the political process has broken down, and the economic process never really got a chance to develop, it is my hope that these small, seemingly modest attempts at cultural and educational dialogue will keep the delicate flame of peacework going, and that they will be joined by others, eventually spreading a light across the Middle East. At the height of the violence around Gaza, I received a depressing email from a friend without hope, and in my reply I wrote that there is nothing we can do about the political situation. 'Let's just bury our heads in the sand and carry on doing Permaculture, bringing Israelis and Palestinians together to heal our damaged environment. We must never give up hope, however unrealistic it may seem.'

I would like to give the last word to Hussein Tarabeah:

> *My first thought was to establish an ecological demonstration centre which would operate as a closed loop, with treated wastewater going for irrigation, biogas going for energy production and sludge for compost. I saw the project as a bridge for peace between Jews and Arabs, Israel and the neighbouring countries, and this is exactly what happened.*
>
> *We took the lead in initiating and advancing a multitude of projects and the fifty thousand visitors every year at our demonstration centre attest to our success. What better tribute than to know that even under the most difficult political circumstances, meetings between Palestinians and Israelis continued at our centre.*
>
> *Every day is a new day for me. My vision is we will continue the momentum that has already been initiated and promote co-operation and dialogue which will bring peace between person and person, between people and the environment.*
>
> (Abbreviated quote first published in the *Israel Environmental Bulletin,* Volume 32, May 2007.)

Jan Martin Bang, Sakhnin, June 2008

Organizations supporting the Sakhnin Centre (TAEQ)

The Centre for Environmental Research and Education of the Towns Association for Environmental Quality (TAEQ) was set up and is supported by the following local authorities:

Sakhnin, Arrabe, Deir Hana, Eilabun, Bu'neina-Nujeidat and Kaukab Abu el-Hija.

It also receives support from:

- The Department for the Protection of the Environment
- The Department of Education
- The Bracha Foundation
- The LIFE Project of the European Union
- The Abraham Foundation
- The Green Environment Foundation
- The Galilee Union/Ford Foundation
- The Nega Trust
- The Oliver Stone Foundation
- The Karov Foundation

References and networking

Because most of the research for this book was done through interviews with the people directly connected to TAEQ, there is no long list of books consulted. It was individuals that we consulted. For those readers who want to follow up and find out more about some of the projects mentioned in the book, here is a list of leads, mostly from the Internet. Happy Hunting!

To learn more about TAEQ:
Towns Association for Environmental Quality
PO Box 1093, Sakhnin, 20173, Israel
www.taeq.org
Tel: +972 4 674 5247

TAEQ's main sponsor:
Israel Ministry of Environmental Protection
www.environment.gov.il

Scientific paper on the wastewater treatment system used at TAEQ:
Tarabia, H., Kimchie, S., Gattas, B. and Sabbah, I. 'Wastewater Treatment And Reclamation In Sakhnin As A Model For Small Communities'. Paper presented at International Workshop on Sewage Treatment and Reuse for Small Communities: Mediterranean and European Experience. Agadir, Morocco, 1996

(Re: the authors, H. Tarabia, of the Regional Environment Protection Unit, Agan Beit Natufa, Sakhnin; S. Kimchie of the Environmental & Water Resources Engineering Division, Technion, Haifa; B. Gattas and I. Sabbah of the R&D Regional Centre, The Galilee Society, Eliabun.)

Maps and atlases of Israel:
www.mapa.co.il

Threefolding:
Steiner, Rudolf, *Towards Social Renewal: Rethinking the Basis of Society*, Rudolf Steiner Press, 1999, ISBN 9781855840720

Permaculture basic text:
Mollison, Bill, *Permaculture — A Designers' Manual.* Tagari Publications, 1988, ISBN 0908228015

Permaculture in Israel:
www.permacultureisrael.org
www.kibbutzlotan.com/creativeEcology/ecoUpdates
www.yevulim-farm.co.il
giladmargalit2@gmail.com
drarbib@gmail.com
yaarbooks@gmail.com

Life and Environment umbrella association:
www.sviva.net

Israel Bio Organic Agriculture Association:
Hachashmonaim Street 121
Tel Aviv 67011, Israel
www.organic-israel.org.il

MED-ENEC:
www.med-enec.com

Tamera Solar Village:
www.tamera.org

The Arava Institute for Environmental Studies:
www.arava.org